T0374591

The Canterbury and York Society

GENERAL EDITOR: A. K. McHARDY

M.A. D.Phil.

ISSN 0262-995X

DIOCESE OF
COVENTRY AND LICHFIELD

CANTERBURY AND YORK SOCIETY VOL. LXXVII

The Register of
John Catterick

BISHOP OF COVENTRY AND LICHFIELD

1415–1419

EDITED BY

R. N. SWANSON

The Canterbury and York Society

The Boydell Press

1990

A Canterbury and York Society publication
First published 1990 by The Boydell Press
an imprint of Boydell & Brewer Ltd
PO Box 9, Woodbridge, Suffolk IP12 3DF
and of Boydell & Brewer Inc.
PO Box 41026, Rochester, NY 14604, USA

British Library Cataloguing in Publication Data
Catholic Church: *Diocese of Coventry and Lichfield, Bishop. 1415–1419 : Catterick.*
1. Catholic Church, Diocese of Coventry and Lichfield. Episcopal services, history
I. Title   II. Swanson, R. N. (Robert Norman)   III. Series
262.0242468
ISBN 0-907239-35-8

Library of Congress Cataloging-in-Publication Data
Catholic Church. Diocese of Coventry and Lichfield (England). Bishop (1415–1419: Catrik)
    The register of John Catterick, Bishop of Coventry and Lichfield,
1415–1419 / edited by R. N. Swanson.
        p.   cm. — (Canterbury and York Society, ISSN 0262-995X; vol. 77)
    Title on ser. t.p.: Diocese of Coventry and Lichfield.
    Includes index.
    ISBN 0-907239-35-8 (alk. paper)
    1. Catholic Church. Diocese of Coventry and Lichfield (England)—History—
Sources.   2. Coventry Region (England)—Church history—Sources.
3. Lichfield Region (England)—Church history—Sources.   4. Church records
and registers—England—Coventry Region.   5. Church records and registers—
England—Lichfield Region.   6. Catrik, John, d. 1419—Manuscripts.   I. Catrik,
John, d. 1419.   II. Swanson, R. N. (Robert Norman)   III. Title.   IV. Title:
Diocese of Coventry and Lichfield.   V. Series: Canterbury and York Society
(Series) ; v. 77.
BX5013.C3A5   vol. 77
[BR763.C825]
283'.41 s—dc20
[282'.424]   90-36641

Details of previous volumes available from Boydell & Brewer

This publication is printed on acid-free paper

Photoset by Rowland Phototypesetting Ltd, Bury St Edmunds, Suffolk
Printed in Great Britain by
St Edmundsbury Press Ltd, Bury St Edmunds, Suffolk

FOR
JOHN AND
ELIZABETH

CONTENTS

		page
Introduction		ix
Abbreviations		xiv
VICAR GENERAL'S COMMISSION		1
ARCHDEACONRY OF COVENTRY		1
ARCHDEACONRY OF DERBY..		10
ARCHDEACONRY OF STAFFORD..		15
ARCHDEACONRY OF SHREWSBURY		18
ARCHDEACONRY OF CHESTER		21
DISPENSATIONS AND DIVERSE LETTERS		24
ORDINATIONS		34
INDEX		69

INTRODUCTION

John Catterick was appointed to the see of Coventry and Lichfield by Pope John XXIII on 1 February 1415. It was not his first episcopal appointment. Some nine months earlier, in April 1414, the same pope had promoted him to the bishopric of St David's, and he had received consecration from the pope himself at Bologna in June. The death of John Burghill in 1414 had released the see of Lichfield. Catterick received his temporalities as bishop of Lichfield in May 1415.

During his tenure of the see, Catterick was for the most part non-resident. His career was essentially that of a curialist, and specifically that of a diplomat. Although he presumably visited his diocese for enthronement (but no mention of that ceremony survives), and it is possible to document his presence within the bishopric on two different occasions, most of the administration was left in the hands of a vicar general, Walter Bullok. When in England Catterick seems to have stayed for the most part in London. But for much of the time he was not even in England. Having come back to England from the Council of Constance on his appointment as bishop of Lichfield, he returned to that assembly in late summer or early autumn of 1416, and remained abroad for the rest of his tenure of the see. In 1417 he was suggested as a possible successor to Robert Hallum in the bishopric of Salisbury, but it was not until late November 1419 that he was actually translated to another diocese – and not to Salisbury, but Exeter. He can scarcely have had time to accustom himself to a new title, as he died, in Florence, only a few weeks later, on 28 December.[1]

The register

The register which covers Catterick's tenure of the see of Lichfield is now deposited at the Lichfield Joint Record Office, as B/A/1/8.[2] In reality, it is not the bishop's register proper, but that of his vicar general. As it survives it is not a lengthy volume, containing a mere forty-five folios. It has suffered some wear, and a number of the marginal titles have been damaged. However, the main body of text on the folios is unaffected. Nevertheless, the register even as it stands is clearly incomplete. A few entries break off in the middle, at the bottom of a page, suggesting that some folios have been lost. There are also other reasons for challenging the completeness of the registration.

Following the customary Lichfield practice, the register divides into two parts, the first being a register of institutions and exchanges; the second a register of

[1] For the careers of Bullok and Catterick, see A. B. Emden, *A biographical register of the university of Oxford to 1500* (3 vols., Oxford, 1957–9), i, pp. 303–4, 371–2.

[2] For a description of the register, see D. M. Smith, *A guide to bishops' registers of England and Wales: a survey from the middle ages to the abolition of episcopacy in 1646* (London, 1981), p. 58. For the earlier registers of the see, see ibid., pp. 54–8.

dispensations, ordinations, and other miscellaneous business. The first half follows the usual practice of registration by archdeaconry, with a separate section for each of the jurisdictions. The second register (which begins at f. 23r) has one section which is essentially of dispensations, and another of ordinations. Notable omissions from this second section are the more ephemeral administrative acts usually to be found in episcopal registers: the letters dimissory, licences for non-residence, and licences for private oratories. This is a major break from earlier Lichfield practice. Beginning in the pontificate of Roger Northburgh (1322–58), when the first signs of the compilation of such a segment for the register are discernible, all Lichfield registers up to and including that of John Burghill, Catterick's immediate predecessor, had contained such a section. From this point on, however, there seem to be few such acts recorded, even if the section of miscellaneous letters remains a lengthy one. It is most unlikely that no such licences were issued at all, but registration practice had clearly altered.

Considering that this register is one compiled for a vicar general, it poses a number of problems. These especially relate to its compilation, and problems of omission. Unlike most registers of vicars general, this is not a straightforward chronological record of acts, but is modelled on the practices adopted in full scale bishops' registers. This suggests one of two possibilities: that Catterick knew on his appointment that he was unlikely to be resident much within the see, and ordered his vicar general to make appropriate allowances in his registration practices; or else that the register is in fact a late compilation, with registration not occurring until some time after the events recorded had actually taken place. The latter suggestion is strongly supported by the arrangement of the documents in the register, which is frequently anything but orderly. Whereas the ordinations do maintain a strict chronological sequence – which is in itself not surprising, since they were performed by suffragan bishops who presumably had their own register of acts from which this ordered series could be transcribed – the organisation of institutions, and some of the dispensations, is chaotic. This suggests that the register was drawn up from the piles of original documents maintained in the registry, but which had been thrown into some disorder whilst awaiting registration. The frequent dating by the 'year as above' also poses problems, especially when a document clearly dated to the January–March period in one year is followed by one dated to another month 'anno ut supra'. I have usually assumed that the scribe meant what he had written, and that the year number was intended to be the same.

In one instance, this system of dating suggests that Bullok may have been overseeing the diocesan administration before the official issue of his commission.[3] This reflects the overall continuity of his activity, for the commission as vicar general did not in reality mark a new appointment. With William de Neuport, Walter Bullok had been commissioned by Archbishop Henry Chichele of Canterbury as keeper of spiritualities during the vacancy of the see following the death of John Burghill.[4] The calendar of the vacancy *acta* in Chichele's register

[3] No. 44.

[4] *The register of Henry Chichele, archbishop of Canterbury, 1414–1443*, ed. E. F. Jacob (Canterbury and York society, vols. 42, 45–7, Oxford, 1937–47), iii, pp. 291–2.

indicates clearly that much of the administration was performed by Bullok alone,[5] and there is evident continuity between his administration *sede vacante*, and as vicar general. Indeed, the later stages of the vacancy register to some extent present a mirror image of the confusion at the start of his time as vicar general: some of the documents were clearly processed after he had been appointed vicar general, with institutions being registered among the vacancy material as late as September 1415.[6] The confusion between functions is admirably reflected in an exchange of benefices which occurred in June 1415, and for which Bullok provided the certificate. The commission for the exchange was addressed from the bishop of Lincoln to Catterick as bishop of Coventry and Lichfield; it was replied to by Bullok as keeper of spiritualities *sede vacante*.[7]

Finally, in dealing with the register, the possibility has to be faced that this may not have been the sole record maintained for Catterick's pontificate. The present register records only three instances of action by the bishop in person: the appointment of Bullok as vicar general; the appointment of an archdeacon of Stafford (no. 122), and in the first of the ordination ceremonies, a strong suggestion that the commission to the suffragan had in that instance been issued by the bishop himself (no. 219). However, it is clear that these are not the sole actions carried out by the bishop in his capacity as diocesan. The (unfortunately incomplete) record of chapter acts for Lichfield during this pontificate mentions a few of his letters. Some of these are clearly induction mandates relating to cathedral dignities, the prebends of Ryton, Prees, Freeford, and Bobenhull; all of them would have been dated within the early months of his pontificate.[8] Unfortunately, the references to the letters do not include full dating, and it is impossible to know whence they were sent. There is evidence for Catterick's involvement in matters affecting his diocese whilst at London in the summer of 1416. From there he issued a dispensation not recorded in the register;[9] and in July 1416 was also one of the actors in the process for the appropriation of Austrey church, Warwickshire, to the abbey of Burton-on-Trent, a process which necessitated correspondence with Bullok within the diocese.[10] If the induction

[5] ibid., iii, pp. 291–347.

[6] ibid., iii, p. 339.

[7] ibid., iii, pp. 339–40.

[8] Lichfield Joint Record Office, D30/I, ff.87–88v. There is a gap in the chronology of the act book from early 1418 to 1424 (ibid., f.99v).

[9] British Library, Add. ch. 77839 (dated at the bishop's lodgings in London, 27 June 1416): a dispensation to confirm the marriage between Thomas Holes and Aleysa, widow of William de Brereton, they having married despite their awareness of the impediment of their relationship in the fourth and fourth degrees of affinity. The dispensation is attached to the original penitentiary commission (Add. ch. 77838), issued by Jordan [Orsini], bishop of Albano, on 1 April 1416 at Constance.

[10] Staffordshire Record Office, D603/ADD/A/639. Bullok's commission to hold the inquiry is dated at London, 14 July 1416, his reply from Burton-on-Trent on 23 July, and the decree of appropriation dated at London, 31 July 1416.

mandates for the prebends (and any other commissions) were issued whilst Catterick was outside his diocese, he may well have compiled his own register of acts. Moreover, even though he was so little within his diocese, it would not be impossible for there to have been another – necessarily very slim – register of his acts whilst the authority of the vicar general was inhibited. Two appointments of secular officials recorded in the chapter acts place the bishop at his manor of Haywood on 8 October 1415, and on 8 June 1416.[11] Assuming that the bishop's presence within the diocese did inhibit the vicar general's authority, this implies at least two visits during which he could have registered his own deeds.

Even allowing for these possibilities, there is other clear evidence that the surviving record for these years is incomplete. The chapter acts indicate several commissions issued by the vicar general which are unrecorded in the register; and occasional evidence from other registers – most notably when dealing with exchanges of benefices – suggests other gaps.[12] Clearly, this is a register with manifold faults, all of which need to be borne in mind when its data are considered.

The calendar

In this calendar, all entries in the register proper have been assigned individual numbers and have been calendared in English. I have ignored the later index which precedes the body of the register, and also a few later fifteenth-century documents transcribed on the rear flyleaves which have nothing to do with Catterick's episcopate. Usually the format of the entries is so standardised that full transcription would have been a pointless luxury. Where there are significant deviations from the standard format, these are indicated either by retention of the appropriate phrase(s), or by a suitable alteration in the method of calendaring. In the abstracts, placenames are generally given in their modern form in the text, but

[11]   Lichfield Joint Record Office, D30/I, ff.92v, 98r–v. In fact, in the last case the duration of the visit can be limited: Catterick was in London on 6 June 1416 (ibid., f.92r), again back there by 27 June (see note 9).

[12]   The Lichfield chapter act book (ibid., ff.92v, 99v) indicates appointments by the vicar general to the prebendal vicarage of Longdon in October 1416, and of a treasurer of Lichfield in March 1418. The first of these omissions causes slight problems: according to Hamilton Thompson, the exchange of which it was part was effected by the bishop of Coventry on commission from the bishop of Lincoln, the corresponding institution to the vicarage of Lilbourne taking place on 16 October (A. H. Thompson, *The abbey of St Mary of the meadows, Leicester* [Leicester, 1949], p. 173). But the entry in the Lichfield act book clearly refers to a commission for the induction of the vicar of Longdon having been issued by the vicar general. The registers of Henry Bowet at York provide other instances of omitted exchanges: in August 1415, of the church of Bradley for that of Tuxford, and in May 1418 an exchange of Ladbrooke for Scrayingham (Borthwick Institute of Historical Research, Reg. 17, f.234r–v, Reg. 18, f.189r–v). For the problems which result from such inter-diocesan exchanges, see N. A. H. Lawrance, '"Foreign" exchanges in the East Riding', *Yorkshire Archaeological Journal*, 42 (1967–70), p. 56. At least one exchange within the diocese is incompletely registered (see no. 21).

the versions given in the register are recorded in the index. The few unmodernised placenames retained in the text are italicised. Surnames are throughout given as in the original, variants within a document being brought together at the first mention of the surname. Variants between documents are collected in the index. All dates between 1 January and 24 March have been indicated by using both old and new style, thus: 2 February 1416/17. Because of the chronological disorder of the register, where the date is indicated by a mere 'anno ut supra' with no clear check against it (i.e., being dated thus at the end of a certificate which includes another document with a clear year), I have placed what I take to be the appropriate year within square brackets, []. Other editorial additions or insertions are also enclosed in [].

The following points should be noted about the individual entries in the calendar:

i. In the institutions, I have omitted the reference to admission. Although this is meticulously recorded, and is technically different from institution, the one could not occur without the other. I have also omitted the reference to the induction mandate where it was issued to the archdeacon of that archdeaconry or his official, as was usually the case. In the identification of patrons, I have dropped the description as 'noble', which is applied to everyone from esquire upwards. I have also omitted the description of vicarages and chantries as perpetual. There appear to be no references to any such posts which were not.

ii. In listing the ordinations, I have simply presented the data as recorded in the register. Most of the references to letters dimissory make the point that they had been granted by the ordinand's diocesan; in a few instances they merely state that he was from a particular diocese, 'etc.'. In such instances, I have standardised as with the fuller description, merely stating that he was ordained 'by l.d.'. The names of the religious houses in the lists have also been amended in the cases of St Thomas near Stafford and the nuns near Derby: in the calendar they are respectively listed as Baswich and Kingsmead.

Acknowledgements

I am grateful to the Lichfield Joint Record Office for providing a microfilm of the register, from which the original calendar was drawn up, and to the staff there for their attention on my occasional visits. The calendar is published by permission of the Diocesan Registrar. Dr R. A. Davies, Dr C. C. Dyer, and Dr M. Gelling kindly assisted with the identification of some of the more elusive place names, and Dr. N. H. Bennett helped with the proofs. Any faults that remain – whether in substance or in typing – are entirely my own responsibility.

R.N.S.
University of Birmingham

ABBREVIATIONS

A. and C.	abbot and convent
abp.	archbishop
Ass. and C.	abbess and convent
B.Dec.	Bachelor of Decrees
B.Theol.	Bachelor of Theology
bp.	bishop
br.	brother
dioc.	in/of the diocese of
esq.	esquire
I.U.D.	Doctor of both laws
kal.	kalends
knt.	knight
l.d.	letters dimissory
lic. leg.	licenciate in laws
LL.B.	Bachelor of Law
LL.D.	Doctor of Law
M.	Master
O.Carm.	Carmelite Order
O.Carth.	Carthusian Order
O.E.S.A.	Order of Augustinian Hermits
O.F.M.	Order of Friars Minor (Franciscans)
O.P.	Order of Preachers (Dominicans)
O.S.A.	Order of St Augustine (hermits are not usually distinguished from canons)
P. and C.	prior and convent
Pss. and C.	prioress and convent
t.	title (for ordination) derived from/provided by

[f.1r] REGISTRUM VENERABILIS VIRI MAGISTRI WALTERI BULLOK, IN LEGIBUS LICENTIATI, ECCLESIE CATHEDRALI LICHFELDENSIS CANONICI, REVERENDI IN CHRISTO PATRIS ET DOMINI, DOMINI JOHANNIS, DEI GRACIA COVENTRENSIS ET LICHFELDENSIS EPISCOPI, IPSO REVERENDO PATRE IN REMOTIS ABGENTE, VICARII IN SPIRITUALIBUS GENERALIS SUFFICIENTER ET LEGITIME DEPUTATI, INCEPTUM VICESIMO PRIMO DIE MENSIS JUNII, ANNO DOMINI MILLESIMO QUADRINGENTESIMO QUINTO DECIMO.

1.   Commission from John [Catterick], bp. of Coventry and Lichfield, to Walter Bullok, canon of Lichfield, appointing him official principal and vicar general in spirituals, with authority to deal with and determine court cases in the consistory of Lichfield or elsewhere within the diocese as yet undetermined or to be brought; to admit, institute, and induct suitable persons who shall be presented to benefices vacant or to be vacant, and to benefices at episcopal collation within the church of Lichfield or elsewhere; to receive resignations for reasons of exchange, and investigate and process such exchanges; to investigate and confirm elections of religious and receive their obedience; to grant letters dimissory and to commission bishops (whether of the realm of England or elsewhere, so long as they received their office from the apostolic see) to carry out ordinations to all orders at the due times; to hold (or cause to be held) examinations of ordinands; and do all else pertaining to the spiritual jurisdiction of the diocese. Winchester, 1 June, 1415.

ARCHDEACONRY OF COVENTRY

2.   [f.1r–v] Institution of Richard Hayward, chaplain, to the vicarage of Wolfhamcote, patron: dean and chapter of St Mary, Warwick, with the obligation of personal residence in accordance with the constitutions of Otto and Ottobono. He offered obedience. Lichfield, 19 January 1416/17.

3.   [f.1v] Institution of Richard Clare to the perpetual chantry founded by M. Philip Turvill, lately canon of Lichfield, in the chapel of St Mary in the parish church of Bedworth. Patrons: P. and C. of Arbury. He swore obedience, and to observe the statutes and ordinances in accordance with the foundation. Lichfield, 9 March 1416/17.

4.   [f.1v–2r] Certificate from the vicar general to Philip [Repingdon], bp. of Lincoln, reciting a commission from that bp. to the bp. of Lichfield (dated at Sleaford Castle, 10 March 1415/16), to inquire into the proposed exchange of benefices between John Racheford, vicar of Great Packington, dioc. Lichfield, and William Hervy, master or warden of Wyham college, dioc. Lincoln, with its annexed chapel of Cadeby; with authority to receive Hervy's resignation and

1

institute Racheford to the mastership on the presentation of Walter Tailboys, Richard Hannsard, John de Fulnetby, Thomas Bukton, clerk, John Bayons, and John West, rector of Biscathorpe, in accordance with the ordination of the college, reserving induction thereto to the bishop of Lincoln. The commission had been fulfilled. Sealed with the seal of the Officiality of the consistory of Lichfield. Lichfield, 31 March 1416.

5.   [f.2r] Institution of William Hervy, chaplain, to the vicarage of Great Packington, vacant by reason of the resignation offered by John Racheford into the hands of the vicar general for an exchange, and after investigation thereof made by the vicar general on his own authority and by commission from Philip [Repingdon], bp. of Lincoln. Patrons: P. and C. of Kenilworth. 31 March 1416.

6.   Institution of John Racheford, in accordance with the above commission, to the college of Wyham with its annexed chapel of Cadeby, dioc. Lincoln, vacant by the resignation of William Hervy offered in the hands of the vicar general for an exchange for the vicarage of Great Packington, as above. Patrons: Walter Tailboys, Richard Hannsard, John de Fulnetby, Thomas Bubton, John Bayens, and John West, rector of Biscathorpe. Same date and place as above.

7.   Institution of Reginald Carix, chaplain, to the vicarage of Offchurch, vacant by the resignation of Hugh Ruhale, offered in the hands of the vicar general in exchange for the vicarage of Wolfhamcote, which had been approved. Patrons: P. and C. of Coventry cathedral. He swore obedience and continual residence. Lichfield, 15 March 1415/16.

8.   Institution of Hugh Ruhale, chaplain, to the vicarage of Wolfhamcote vacant by the resignation offered by Reginald Carix in the hands of the vicar general in exchange for the vicarage of Offchurch, which had been approved. Patrons: dean and chapter of St Mary, Warwick. He swore obedience and continual residence. Date and place as above.

9.   Institution of Alexander Sherman, chaplain, to the vicarage of Clifton on Dunsmore, vacant by the resignation of John Whatton. Patrons: A. and C. of St Mary de Pratis, Leicester. He swore obedience and continual residence. Lichfield, 27 April, [1415].

10.   [f.2v] Institution of Thomas Thurston, chaplain, to the rectory of Rugby, vacant by the resignation of Richard Hosell. Patrons: A. and C. of St Mary de Pratis, Leicester. He swore obedience. Lichfield, 20 April 1417.

11.   Institution of William Aleyn, chaplain, to the church of Baxterley. Patron for this turn: Thomas del Asteley of Appleby, esq. He swore obedience. Lichfield, 26 June 1415.

12.   Certificate of the vicar general to Philip [Repingdon], bp. of Lincoln, reciting a commission from that bp. to the bp. of Coventry and Lichfield or his vicar general (dated at Sleaford Castle, 18 June 1416), to inquire into a proposed

exchange of benefices between Alexander Benet, rector of Avon Dassett, and John Excetre, rector of Fenny Drayton, dioc. Lincoln, with authority to receive John's resignation and institute Alexander to Fenny Drayton (patrons: P. and C. of Jesus of Bethlehem near Sheen, O. Carth.), but reserving his induction and oath of canonical obedience. The commission had been fulfilled. Lichfield, 25 June 1416.

13.   [f.3r] Institution of John Excetre, chaplain, to the rectory of Avon Dassett, vacant by the resignation offered to the vicar general by Alexander Benet for the above exchange, which had been approved on his own authority and that of Philip [Repingdon], bp. of Lincoln. Patron: William Monford, lord of Coleshill. Lichfield, 25 June 1416.

14.   Institution of Alexander Benet, chaplain, by virtue of the above commission, to the church of Fenny Drayton, dioc. Lincoln, vacant by the resignation offered by John Excetre to the vicar general in exchange for the church of Avon Dassett, which had been approved. Patrons: P. and C. of Jesus of Bethlehem near Sheen. Same date and place as above.

15.   [f.3r–v] Certificate of the vicar general to Philip [Repingdon], bp. of Lincoln, reciting a commission from that bp. to the bp. of Coventry and Lichfield or his vicar general (dated at Sleaford Castle, 23 June 1416), to inquire into a proposed exchange of benefices between William Hervy, vicar of Great Packington, and John Shylton, vicar of St Nicholas, Leicester, dioc. Lincoln, with authority to receive John's resignation and institute William to St Nicholas (patrons: A. and C. of St Mary de Pratis, Leicester), with the obligations of personal ministration and continual residence, in accordance with the constitutions of Otto and Ottobono, but reserving his induction and the oath of canonical obedience. The commission had been fulfilled. Lichfield, 26 June 1416.

16.   [f.3v] Institution of William Hervy, chaplain, to the vicarage of Great Packington, vacant by the resignation offered by John Shylton to the vicar general in an exchange approved by him, on his own authority and that of Philip [Repingdon], bp. of Lincoln. Patrons: P. and C. of Kenilworth. He swore obedience and continual residence. Lichfield, 26 June 1416.

17.   Institution, by virtue of the above commission, of John Shylton, chaplain, to the vicarage of St Nicholas, Leicester, dioc. Lincoln, vacant by the resignation offered by William Hervy to the vicar general in exchange for the vicarage of Great Packington, which had been approved. Patrons: A. and C. of St Mary de Pratis, Leicester. He swore obedience and continual residence. Same date and place as above.

18.   [ff.3v–4r] Certificate of the vicar general to Philip [Repingdon], bp. of Lincoln, reciting a commission from that bp. to the bp. of Coventry and Lichfield or his vicar general (dated at Sleaford Castle, 1 June 1417), to inquire into a proposed exchange of benefices between Nicholas de Croxale, vicar of Bickenhill, and William Bikenhull, rector of Saxby, dioc. Lincoln, with authority to receive

William's resignation and institute Nicholas to Saxby (patron for that turn: Thomas Chaworth, knt.), but reserving his induction and oath of canonical obedience. The commission had been fulfilled. Lichfield, 3 June 1417.

19.   [f.4r] Institution of William Bikenhull, chaplain, to the vicarage of Bickenhill, vacant by the resignation offered by Nicholas Croxhale to the vicar general for an exchange approved by him on his own authority and that of Philip [Repingdon], bp. of Lincoln. Patrons: Pss. and C. of Markyate. He swore obedience and continual residence. Lichfield, 3 June 1417.

20.   Institution, by virtue of the above commission, of Nicholas Croxale to the rectory of Saxby, dioc. Lincoln, vacant by the resignation offered by William Bikenhull to the vicar general in exchange for the vicarage of Bickenhill, which he had approved. Patron: Thomas Chaworth, knt. Same date and place as above.

21.   Institution of William Clerk, chaplain, to the rectory of Wishaw, vacant by the resignation offered by John Rolf to the vicar general in exchange for the vicarage of Hathersage, which had been approved. Patron: Elizabeth, widow of Baldwin Bereford. Lichfield, 23 July, [1417].

22.   Institution of Richard Assheby, chaplain, to the church of Leek Wootton. Patrons: P. and C. of Kenilworth. 31 July, [1417].

23.   [f.4r–v] Certificate to the vicar general from James Walsyngham, lic. leg., vicar general for John [Wakeryng], bp. of Norwich, reciting a commission from the vicar general to that bp. (dated at Lichfield, 15 September 1416, and sealed with the seal of the Officiality of the consistory of Lichfield) to inquire into the proposed exchange of benefices between William Palmer, rector of Elmdon, and John Tudde, rector of St Peter, Southgate, Norwich, giving him authority to receive William's resignation and institute John to Elmdon (patron: Joanna Waldyns, lady of Elmdon), but reserving his induction and oath of canonical obedience. The commission had been fulfilled. Norwich, 25 September 1416.

24.   [f.4v] Institution of Thomas Botyler, chaplain, to the vicarage of Harbury. Patrons: P. and C. of Kenilworth. He swore obedience and continual residence. 21 August, [1416].

25.   Repeat of no. 8, now dated at Lichfield, 19 March, [1416/17].

26.   [f.5r] Institution of M. Gregory Newport, B.Dec., to the church of Church Lawford. Patrons: P. and C. of St Anne near Coventry, O. Carth. Lichfield, 7 September 1416.

27.   Certificate of the vicar general to Philip [Repingdon], bp. of Lincoln, reciting a commission from that bp. to the bp. of Coventry and Lichfield or his vicar general (dated at Sleaford Castle, 22 August 1416), to inquire into a proposed exchange of benefices between John Islep, vicar of Bishops Itchington, and Thomas Flessher, rector of Newton Purcell, dioc. Lincoln, with authority to

receive Thomas's resignation and institute John or his proctor to Newton Purcell (patrons: P. and C. of Bicester), reserving his induction and oath of canonical obedience. The commission had been fulfilled. Lichfield, 1 September 1416.

28. Institution of Thomas Flessher, chaplain, to the vicarage of Bishops Itchington, vacant by the resignation of John Islep offered to the vicar general in exchange for the church of Newton Purcell, dioc. Lincoln. Patron: Robert Wolden, precentor of Lichfield cathedral and prebendary of Bishops Itchington. 1 September, 1416.

29. Institution of John Islep to the church of Newton Purcell by virtue of the above exchange. Patrons: P. and C. of Bicester. Same date and place as above.

30. Institution of William Prestwode, chaplain, to the hospital of St Thomas the Martyr, Birmingham. Patron: Elizabeth de Clynton. 26 October, [1416].

31. [f.5v] Institution of John Mason, chaplain, to the vicarage of Newnham, vacant by the resignation of Thomas Wryght. Patrons: P. and C. of Kenilworth. He swore obedience and continual residence. Lichfield, 22 July, [1417].

32. Institution of Robert Sturdy, clerk, to the rectory of Southam, vacant by the resignation of M. John Besevile. Patron for this turn: M. William Glymme, vicar of St Michael, Coventry. He swore obedience, and to maintain without interruption the payment of an annual pension of £20 from the revenues of the church to the dean and chapter of Lichfield cathedral, at the times and places set out fully in the agreement. Coventry, 10 September 1417.

33. Institution of Richard Watton, chaplain, to the vicarage of Radway. Patrons: A. and C. of Stoneleigh. He swore obedience and continual residence. 28 September, [1417].

34. Institution of William Screyfeld, chaplain, to the vicarage of Grand-borough, vacant by the resignation of John Hildys. Patrons: P. and C. of Ranton. He swore obedience and continual residence. 8 October, [1417].

35. Institution of William Clyfton, chaplain, to the vicarage of Stoneleigh. Patrons: P. and C. of St Mary, Kenilworth. He swore obedience and continual residence. 23 October, [1417].

36. Institution of John Longlee, chaplain, in the person of Thomas Stonley, clerk, his proctor, to the chantry founded by M. Philip Turvill, formerly canon of Lichfield cathedral, in the chapel of St Mary in the parish church of Bedworth. Patrons: P. and C. of Arbury. The proctor swore obedience, and to observe the statutes and ordinances of the chantry according to its foundation. 25 October, [1417].

37. [ff.5v–6r] Institution of Nicholas Crosseby, chaplain, in the person of John Boidell, esq., his proctor, to a mediety of the church of Ufton, which is taken to be a prebend in Lichfield cathedral, vacant by the death of M. Hugh Holbache,

the last prebendary. Patrons: P. and C. of Coventry cathedral. At the same date and place the dean and chapter [of Lichfield] were mandated to induct him, and to assign him the stall in choir and place in chapter traditionally linked with the prebend. 26 October, [1417].

38.　　[f.6r] Certificate of the vicar general to M. Richard Bruton, chancellor of Wells cathedral, and vicar general for Richard [Clifford], bp. of London, reciting a commission from him to the bp. of Coventry and Lichfield or his vicar general (dated at London, 15 November 1416) to inquire into a proposed exchange of benefices between John Bote, chaplain of the chantry founded at the altar of St Mary the Virgin in the church of St Michael Cornhill in the city of London for the souls of Robert Newcomen, Matilda and Petronilla his wives, his brothers, sisters, relatives, and all the faithful departed, and John Whiteacre, rector of Stockton, with authority to receive Bote's resignation and institute Whiteacre to the chantry (patron for this turn: John Pecche, esq.), after he had sworn to observe the ordination of the chantry, and reserving his induction and canonical obedience. The commission had been fulfilled. London, 16 November 1416, using the seal at hand ('quod ad manus habemus').

39.　　[f.6r–v] Institution of John Bote, chaplain, to the rectory of Stockton, vacant by the resignation offered by John Whiteacre to the vicar general in exchange for the chantry in the church of St Michael Cornhill in the city of London, which he had approved on his own authority and that of M. Richard Bruton, vicar general for Richard [Clifford], bp. of London. Patrons: P. and C. of Hertford. 16 November, [1416].

40.　　[f.6v] Institution of John Whiteacre, chaplain, by virtue of the above commission, to the chantry in the church of St Michael Cornhill in the city of London, vacant by the resignation offered by John Bote to the vicar general in exchange for the church of Stockton as above. Patron for this turn: John Pecche, esq. Same date and place as above.

41.　　Institution of William Smyth, chaplain, to the church of Harborough Magna. Patron: Adam de Pesale, knt. He swore obedience. 8 November, [1416].

42.　　Institution of M. Thomas Cristenmasse, B.Theol., to the prebend of Milverton in the collegiate church of Astley. Patron: William de Astley, knt., lord of Astley. After he had taken the oath of obedience the mandate was issued for his induction. 13 December 1415.

43.　　Institution of John West, chaplain, to the priestly office of the canon and prebend of Wolvey Astley in the collegiate church of Astley. Patron: M. John Howbell, canon and prebendary of Wolvey Astley. Having sworn obedience, letters for induction were sent to the dean of the place. 18 December, [1415].

44.　　Institution of John Steward, chaplain, to the church of Radbourn. Patron: John Catesby, esq. 27 April, [1415].[1]

　　　[1] 'anno domini supradicto' – which would make it predate Bullok's commission as vicar general (see no. 1). Really 1416?

6

45.   Institution of William Bartlot, chaplain, to the vicarage of Willoughby, vacant by the resignation of John Garsyngton. Patrons: the warden and brethren of the hospital of St John the Baptist outside the east gate of Oxford. He swore obedience and continual residence. 15 October, [1415].

46.   Institution of John Racheford, chaplain, to the vicarage of Leek Wootton, vacant by the resignation of William son of Richard de Assheby. Patrons: P. and C. of Kenilworth. He swore obedience and continual residence. 26 October, [1415].

47.   [f.7r] Institution of John West, chaplain, to the church of Baddesley Clinton. Patron: Joan Burdet, lady of Baddesley. 4 November 1418.

48.   Institution of William Reynald, chaplain, to the vicarage of Radway, vacant by the resignation of Richard Watton. Patrons: A. and C. of Stoneleigh. He swore obedience and continual residence. 22 December, [1418].

49.   Institution of M. Henry Scharyngton, clerk, to the rectory of Wappenbury, vacant by the resignation of M. John Bernard. Patrons: P. and C. of the house of the Visitation of St Mary in the Isle of Axholme, O.Carth., dioc. Lincoln. 24 December, [1418].

50.   [f.7r–v] Certificate of the vicar general to Thomas [Langley], bp. of Durham, reciting a commission from that bp. to the bp. of Coventry and Lichfield or his vicar general (dated at his manor of Old Ford, near London, 5 January 1418/19) to inquire into a proposed exchange of benefices between Robert de Thresk, vicar of St Nicholas, Newcastle upon Tyne, dioc. Durham, and William Glym, vicar of St Michael, Coventry, with authority to receive Robert's resignation and institute William to St Nicholas (patron: William [Strickland], bp. of Carlisle), reserving his induction and canonical obedience. The commission had been fulfilled, an oath having been imposed on William for personal ministration and continual residence in accordance with the constitutions of Otto and Ottobono. Lichfield, 10 January, 1418/19.

51.   [f.7v] Institution of Robert Thresk, chaplain, in the person of John Burton, clerk, his proctor, to the vicarage of St Michael, Coventry, vacant by the resignation offered by William Glym to the vicar general in exchange for the vicarage of St Nicholas, Newcastle upon Tyne, dioc. Durham, which he had approved on his own authority and that of Thomas [Langley], bp. of Durham. Patrons: P. and chapter or C. of the cathedral or conventual church of Coventry. The proctor took the oath of canonical obedience and continual residence. He was granted letters of induction addressed to the archdeacon or his Official. 10 January, [1418/19].

52.   Institution of William Glym, chaplain, by authority of the above commission, to the vicarage of St Nicholas, Newcastle upon Tyne, dioc. Durham, vacant by the resignation offered by Robert Thresk to the vicar general in exchange for the vicarage of St Michael, Coventry, dealt with as above. Patron:

William [Strickland], bp. of Carlisle. He was obliged to personal and continual residence according to the constitutions of Otto and Ottobono. A certificate of the proceedings was sent to the bp. of Durham on the same day. Same date and place as above.

53.   Institution of William Clement, chaplain, to the priestly office of the canonry and prebend of Wolvey Astley in the collegiate church of Astley. Patron: M. John Howbell, canon and prebendary of Wolvey Astley. Having taken the oath of obedience, letters for his induction were sent to the dean of the place. 25 October, [1418].

54.   Institution of Robert Pent, chaplain, to the vicarage of Clifton on Dunsmore, vacant by the resignation of William Smyth. Patrons: A. and C. of St Mary de Pratis, Leicester. He swore obedience and continual residence. 2 March, [1418/19].

55.   [f.8r] Certificate of the vicar general to Philip [Repingdon], bp. of Lincoln, reciting a commission from that bp. to the bp. of Coventry and Lichfield or his vicar general (dated at Sleaford Castle, 28 March 1419) to inquire into a proposed exchange of benefices between John Maryot, dean of the collegiate church of Astley, and Nicholas Wildebore, vicar of Swalcliffe, dioc. Lincoln, with authority to receive Nicholas's resignation and institute John to Swalcliffe (patrons: the warden and fellows of the college of St Mary of Winchester, Oxford), and imposing the oath according to the legatine constitutions, but reserving his induction and canonical obedience. The commission had been fulfilled, with the imposition of oaths of personal ministration and continual residence, in accordance with the constitutions of Otto and Ottobono. Lichfield, 31 March, 1419.

56.   Institution of Nicholas Wildebore to the deanery of the collegiate church of Astley, vacant by the resignation offered by John Maryot to the vicar general for an exchange approved by him on his own authority and that of Philip [Repingdon], bp. of Lincoln. Patron: William de Asteley, knt., lord of Astley. He swore continual residence and personal ministration according to the foundation of the church. 31 March, [1419].

57.   [f.8v] Institution of John Mariot, chaplain, in accordance with the above commission, to the vicarage of Swalcliffe, dioc. Lincoln, vacant by the resignation offered by Nicholas Wildebore to the vicar general in exchange for the deanery of the collegiate church of Astley, as above. Patrons: the warden and fellows of the college of St Mary of Winchester at Oxford. He swore obedience and continual residence. Same date and place, year as below.

58.   Institution of William Tyler, chaplain, to the chantry at the altar of St Mary in the parish church of Hillmorton. Patron: Thomas Asteley, esq., lord of Hillmorton. He swore to observe the statutes and ordinances of the chantry according to the foundation. 2 May 1419.

59.   Institution of Philip Lye, chaplain, to the chantry of St James in the parish church of Hillmorton. Patron: William Coppe of Coventry. He swore to observe the statutes and ordinances of the chantry according to the foundation. 2 May, [1419].

60.   Institution of John West, chaplain, to the vicarage of Polesworth. Patrons: Ass. and C. of Polesworth. He swore obedience and continual residence. 2 August, [1419].

61.   Institution of Robert Fawcus, chaplain, to a mediety of the chantry of Percy in the church of Holy Trinity, Coventry, vacant by the resignation of Thomas Anston. Patron: br. Richard Crosseby, prior of Coventry cathedral. He swore to observe the statutes and ordinances of the chantry according to the foundation. 5 October, [1419].

62.   Institution of M. Richard Leyot, LL.D., in the person of Thomas Rodeley, his proctor, to the vicarage of St Michael, Coventry. Patrons: P. and C. of St Mary, Coventry. The proctor swore obedience and continual residence. 19 November, [1419].

63.   Institution of William Wroo, chaplain, in the person of John Scheryngton, his proctor, to the rectory of Wappenbury, vacant by the resignation of M. Henry Schiryngton. Patrons: P. and C. of the house of the Visitation of St Mary in the Isle of Axholme, dioc. Lincoln. 26 November, [1419].

64.   Institution of Gerard Elys, chaplain, to the vicarage of Scarcliffe. Patrons: A. and C. of St Mary, Darley. He swore obedience and continual residence. Lichfield, 8 January 1416/17.

65.   Institution of William Reresby, chaplain, to the parish church of Ashover. Patron: Thomas Reresby, knt. Coventry, 21 September, [1416].

66.   Institution of William de Hyndeley, chaplain, to the vicarage of Glossop. Patrons: A. and C. of Basingwerk. He swore obedience and continual residence. Lichfield, 14 September, [1416].

67.   Institution of Roger Hayward, chaplain, to the vicarage of Longford. Patron: Richard de Radeclif, rector of Longford. He swore obedience and continual residence. Lichfield, 2 November, [1416].

68.   Institution of Roger Stedman, chaplain, in the person of John Haston, his proctor, to the church of Eyam. Patron: John Talbot, knt., lord Furnival. Lichfield, 6 August 1417.

69.   Institution of br. William Derby, canon, to the vicarage of Alvaston, vacant by the resignation of Robert Fysher. Patrons: P. and C. of Shelford. He swore obedience and continual residence. Derby, 3 September, [1417].

70.   Institution of William de Wylton, chaplain, to the vicarage of Melbourne. Patron: William [Strickland], bp. of Carlisle. He swore obedience and continual residence. Lichfield, 28 January, [1417/18].

71.   Institution of Robert Kyrkeman, chaplain, to the parish church of North Wingfield. Patron: Alice Deyncourt. Lichfield, 20 August 1416.

72.   Institution of Thomas Medburne, chaplain, to the parish church of South Wingfield. Patron: John Bussy, knt., lord of Hougham. Lichfield, 13 June, [1416].

73.   Institution of Richard Whitlombe, chaplain, to the rectory of Kedleston vacant by the resignation of Walter Leykirke. Patron: John Curson, esq. Lichfield, 11 January, [1416/17].

74.   [f.9v] Certificate of the vicar general to Philip [Repingdon], bp. of Lincoln, reciting a commission from that bp. to the bp. of Coventry and Lichfield or his vicar general (dated at Sleaford Castle, 1 March 1415/16), to inquire into a proposed exchange of benefices between William Toneworth, rector of Dalbury, and Robert son of Simon de Bamburgh, rector of Little Gidding, dioc. Lincoln,

with authority to receive Robert's resignation and institute William to Little Gidding (patron: br. Walter Grendon, prior of the Order of St John of Jerusalem in England), reserving his induction and canonical obedience. The commission had been fulfilled. Lichfield, 4 March 1415/16.

75.   Institution of the above Simon ⟨sic⟩ Bamburgh, chaplain, to the rectory of Dalbury, vacant by the resignation of William Toneworth in exchange for the rectory of Little Gidding, dioc. Lincoln. Patron: John, son of John Holand, knt. 4 March, [1415/16].

76.   Institution of William Toneworth to the church of Little Gidding by the above exchange. Patron: br. John ⟨sic⟩ Grendon, prior of the Order of St John of Jerusalem in England. Same date and place as above.

77.   Institution of M. John Pole, clerk, to the church of Brailsford. Patron: the king, in right of his duchy of Lancaster. Lichfield, 9 March 1417/18.

78.   [f.10r] Certificate of the vicar general to Philip [Repingdon], bp. of Lincoln, reciting a commission from that bp. to the bp. of Coventry and Lichfield or his vicar general (dated at Sleaford Castle, 25 January 1416/17), to inquire into a proposed exchange of benefices between John Fouler, rector of Bradley, and John Fridaythorp, vicar of the prebendal church of Sutton le Marsh, dioc. Lincoln, with authority to receive Fridaythorp's resignation and institute Fouler to the vicarage (patron: M. Thomas Duffeld, chancellor of Lincoln cathedral and prebendary of the prebend of Sutton attached to that dignity), and according to the legatine constitutions, reserving his induction and canonical obedience. The commission had been fulfilled, Fouler taking an oath of personal ministration and continual residence in accordance with the constitutions of Otto and Ottobono. Lichfield, 28 January 1416/17.

79.   Institution of John Fridaythorp, chaplain, to the church of Bradley, vacant by the resignation of John Fouler in exchange for the vicarage of the prebendal church of Sutton le Marsh, dioc. Lincoln. Patron: John Macworth, dean of Lincoln cathedral. 28 January, [1416/17].

80.   Institution of John Fouler to the vicarage of the prebendal church of Sutton le Marsh, vacant by the above exchange. Patron: M. Thomas Duffeld, chancellor of Lincoln cathedral and prebendary of Sutton. Same date and place as above.

81.   [f.10v] Certificate of the chapter of York Minster, the dean being absent, reciting a commission to them from the vicar general (dated at Lichfield, 27 April 1417, and sealed with the seal of the consistory of Lichfield) to inquire into a proposed exchange of benefices between John Fridaythorp *alias* Clerk [Clerc], rector of Bradley, and William Begon, vicar of the prebendal church of Friday-thorpe, dioc. York, with authority to receive John's resignation and institute William to Bradley (patron: M. John Macworth, dean of Lincoln cathedral), reserving his induction and canonical obedience. The commission had been fulfilled. York, 7 May 1417.

82.   [ff.10v–11r] Certificate of the vicar general to Henry [Bowet], abp. of York, reciting a commission from that abp. to the bp. of Coventry and Lichfield or his vicar general (dated at Cawood, 28 June 1416) to inquire into a proposed exchange of benefices between William Asshebery, rector of Morton, and John de Hynton, master or warden of the college or chantry of St Mary at Sibthorpe, dioc. York, with authority to receive John's resignation and institute William to the mastership (patron: Thomas Payn, colleague or chaplain of the said college or chantry), with all obligations according to the foundation, and reserving his induction and canonical obedience. The commission had been fulfilled. Lichfield, 2 July 1416.

83.   [f.11r] Institution of John Hynton, chaplain, to the rectory of Morton, vacant by the resignation of William Asshebery in exchange for the college or chantry of St Mary at Sibthorpe, dioc. York. Patron: John Buscy, knt. 2 July, [1416].

84.   Institution of William Asshebery to the college or chantry of St Mary at Sibthorpe, dioc. York, vacant by the above exchange. Patron: Thomas Payn, colleague or chaplain of the said college or chantry. Same date and place as above.

85.   [f.11r–v] Certificate of the vicar general to Henry [Bowet], abp. of York,[1] reciting a commission from that abp. to the bp. of Coventry and Lichfield or his vicar general (dated at Cawood, 4 July 1415) to inquire into the proposed exchange of benefices between John Stapulforth, vicar of Ault Hucknall, and Thomas Lillyng, vicar of Wysall, dioc. York, with authority to receive Thomas's resignation and institute John to Wysall (patrons: P. and C. of Worksop, dioc. York), with the obligation of personal residence in accordance with the constitutions of Otto and Ottobono, and reserving his induction and canonical obedience. The commission had been fulfilled, John having sworn personal ministration and continual residence in accordance with the constitutions. Lichfield, 8 July, [1415].

> [1]   At the first appearance of his name, in the addressing clause of the certificate, his see is erroneously given as Canterbury.

86.   [f.11v] Institution of Thomas Lillyng, chaplain, to the vicarage of Ault Hucknall, vacant by the resignation of John Stapulforth in exchange for the vicarage of Wysall, dioc. York. Patrons: P. and C. of Newstead. He swore obedience and continual residence. Lichfield, 8 July, [1415].

87.   Institution of John Stapulforth, chaplain, to the vicarage of Wysall, dioc. York, by the above exchange. Patrons: P. and C. of Worksop. Same date and place as above.

88.   Institution of John Thurnaston, chaplain, to the chantry of St Katherine in the church of St Michael, Melbourne. Patron: Richard Baro, vicar of Barrow upon Trent. He swore obedience, and to observe the statutes and ordinances of the chantry according to its foundation, saving legitimate impediment. 31 July, [1415].

89.   [f.12r] Institution of Thomas Dauntre, chaplain, to the church of Swarkeston. Patron: William Rolleston, lord of Swarkeston. Lichfield, 12 August, [1415].

90.   Institution of Thomas Stacy, chaplain, to the vicarage of Horsley, vacant by the resignation of John Gylot. Patrons: P. and C. of Lenton. He swore obedience and continual residence. Lichfield, 9 July 1418.

91.   Certificate of the vicar general to Philip [Repingdon], bp. of Lincoln, reciting a commission from that bp. to the bp. of Coventry and Lichfield or his vicar general (dated at Sleaford Castle, 12 April 1418) to inquire into a proposed exchange of benefices between Henry de Bilburgh, rector of Boyleston, and Robert de Germethorpe, rector of a mediety of East Keal, dioc. Lincoln, with authority to receive Robert's resignation and institute Henry to the mediety (patron: br. John Brompston, lieutenant during his absence from England of br. William Hulles, prior of the Order of St John of Jerusalem in England), reserving his induction and canonical obedience. The commission had been fulfilled. Lichfield, 15 April, 1418.

92.   Institution of Robert Germethorp, chaplain, to the rectory of Boyleston, vacant by the resignation of Henry de Bamburgh ⟨sic⟩ in exchange for a mediety of the church of East Keal, dioc. Lincoln. Patron: John Coton of Ridware. 15 April, [1418].

93.   [f.12v] Institution of Henry Bilbourgh ⟨sic⟩, chaplain, to a mediety of the church of East Keal, dioc. Lincoln, by reason of the above exchange. Patron: br. John Brompston, lieutenant during his absence from England for br. William Hulles, prior of the Order of St John of Jerusalem in England. Same date and place as above.

94.   Institution of John by the Kyrke, chaplain, to the church of Sutton Scarsdale. Patron: Humphrey de Halugton, esq. 12 August, 1418.

95.   Institution of Roger Morton, chaplain, to the church of Clowne. Patrons: P. and C. of Worksop. 5 April, [1418].

96.   Institution of M. Robert Takell, LL.B., to the church of Pleasley. Patron for this turn: Thomas Haxey, lord of Pleasley. Chesterfield, 5 April, [1418].

97.   Institution of br. Richard de Ilkeston, canon, to the vicarage of Ilkeston. Patrons: A. and C. of Dale. He swore obedience and continual residence. 17 March, [1418/19].

98.   Institution of Hugh Penyale, chaplain, to the vicarage of Crich, vacant by the resignation of Peter Trusbut. Patrons: A. and C. of Darley. He swore obedience and continual residence. 22 January, [1418/19].

99.   Institution of br. John Stonley, canon, to the vicarage of Kirk Hallam. Patrons: A. and C. of Dale. He swore obedience and continual residence. 1 March, [1418/19].

100.   Institution of Geoffrey Shardelowe, chaplain, to the second chaplaincy of the chantry in the chapel of Chaddesden. Patrons: A. and C. of Darley. He swore to observe the statutes and ordinances of the chantry according to its ordination and foundation. 18 February, [1418/19].

101.   Institution of Roger Power, chaplain, to the vicarage of Heath. Patrons: A. and C. of Croxton. He swore obedience and continual residence. 2 May, [1418].

102.   Institution of William Mason, chaplain, to the vicarage of Alstone. Patrons: A. and C. of Croxden. He swore obedience and continual residence. Lichfield, 18 February 1415/16.

103.   Institution of M. John Stafford, professor of civil law, to the rectory of Clifton Campville, vacant by the resignation of Laurence Haukyn. Patron: Edmund [Stafford], bp. of Exeter, lord of the lordship and manor of Clifton Campville. Lichfield, 22 February, [1415/16].

104.   Institution of William Person, chaplain, to the vicarage of Dilhorne. Patrons: the dean and chapter of Lichfield. He swore obedience and continual residence. 23 April 1416.

105.   Institution of William Witherley, clerk, to the rectory of Thorpe Constantine, vacant by the resignation of Richard Witherley. Patron: the king. 30 November 1417.

106.   Institution of Thomas Shirley, chaplain, to the vicarage of Ilam, vacant by the resignation of Ralph de Gaunstede. Patrons: A. and C. of Burton on Trent. He swore obedience and continual residence. 4 December, [1417].

107.   [f.13r–v] Certificate to the vicar general from Thomas Cranley, LL.B., rector of Bishops Hatfield and commissary or lieutenant of Thomas [Cranley], abp. of Dublin and primate of Ireland, dean of the royal free chapel of Penkridge, reciting a commission from the vicar general to the dean or his lieutenant (dated at Coventry, 22 September 1416, and sealed with the seal of the Officiality of Lichfield), to inquire into a proposed exchange of benefices between John Reynald, rector of a mediety of Mugginton, and Roger Gybones, prebendary of the prebend called 'regie' in the royal free chapel of Penkridge,[1] with authority to receive John's resignation and admit and institute Roger to the mediety (patron: William de Rolleston, esq.), reserving his induction and oath of obedience. The commission had been fulfilled. Penkridge, 8 October, 1416, sealed with the seal of the jurisdiction.[2]

[1]   The name given in the document is not one usually ascribed to any of the seven prebends established within the chapel.

[2]   This entry is possibly misplaced. Mugginton is in Derbyshire, and the entry ought therefore to appear under that archdeaconry. That Penkridge was within the archdeaconry of Stafford may account for its appearance here; but Penkridge as a royal free chapel fell within a peculiar jurisdiction which was outside the bishop's control, so that it should not affect the organisation of the register.

108.   [f.13v] Institution of Samson Erdeswik, clerk, to the rectory of Kingsley. Patron: Roger de Bradschawe, esq. 16 October, [1416].

109.   Institution of Thomas Admondeston, chaplain, to the rectory of Forton, vacant by the resignation offered by William Corley to the vicar general in exchange for the vicarage of the prebendal church of Prees, which had been approved. Patron: Hugh Burnell, lord of Holdgate and Weoley. 12 January, [1416/17].

110.   Institution of William Corley to the vicarage of the prebendal church of Prees, vacant by reason of the above exchange. Patron: John Forest, canon and prebendary of Prees. He swore obedience and continual residence. The dean and chapter of Lichfield were mandated to induct. Same date and place as above.

111.   Institution of William Russell, chaplain, to the rectory of Norbury. Patron: Philip Boteler, knt., lord of Norbury. 19 February, [1416/17].

112.   Institution of William Jamiesson, chaplain, to the rectory of Darlaston. Patron: Thomas de Dorlaston. 20 October, [1416].

113.   Institution of William Lachefer to the vicarage of Sheriff Hales. Patrons: the house of Jesus of Bethlehem at Sheen, O. Carth. He swore obedience and continual residence. 8 November 1417.

114.   Institution of John Wouburn, clerk, to the rectory of Hanbury. Patron: the king, in right of his duchy of Lancaster. 23 October 1418.

115.   [f.14r] Certificate of the vicar general to Henry [Bowet], abp. of York, reciting a commission from that abp. to the bp. of Coventry and Lichfield or his vicar general (dated at Cawood manor, 15 July 1417) to inquire into a proposed exchange of benefices between Robert Halom, rector of Blore, and John [de] Lowthe, rector of a mediety of Treswell, dioc. York (patrons: Roger Ask and Thomas de Newesone, domicelli), reserving his induction and canonical obedience. The commission had been fulfilled. Lichfield, 22 July, 1417.

116.   Institution of John Lowthe, chaplain, to the rectory of Blore, vacant by the resignation of Robert Halom in exchange for a mediety of the church of Treswell, dioc. York. Patron: Edmund Basset, esq. 22 July, [1417].

117.   Institution of Robert Halom to a mediety of the church of Treswell, dioc. York, vacant by the above exchange. Patrons: Roger Ask and Thomas Neweson. Same date and place as above.

118.   Institution of Nicholas Sondon, chaplain, to the church of Kingsley. Patrons for this turn: John Dedyk and Margaret his wife. 17 October, [1417].

119.   [f.14r–v] Institution of Thomas Savage, clerk, to the church of Checkley. Patron: John Savage, knt. 3 January, [1417/18].

120.   [f.14v] Institution of M. Gregory Neweport to the vicarage of the prebendal church of Eccleshall. Patron: M. Walter Bullok, canon and prebendary of Eccleshall. He swore obedience and continual residence. Lichfield, 15 March 1418/19.

121.   Institution of Thomas Lyot, chaplain, to the vicarage of the prebendal church of Longdon. Patron: M. William Neweport, canon and prebendary of Longdon. He swore obedience and continual residence. The dean and chapter of Lichfield were mandated to induct. 15 April, [1418].

122.   Collation, by the bp., of the archdeaconry of Stafford in Lichfield cathedral to M. John Fytton, B.Theol. The bishop's lodgings, Geneva, 13 July 1418.

123.   Institution of Hugh Carpenter, chaplain, to the chantry of the mass of the Blessed Virgin Mary in Enville church. Patron: Isabella, lady of Lutley. He swore to observe the statutes and ordinances of the chantry according to its foundation. 3 January, [1418/19].

124.   Institution of Robert Shiryngton, in the person of John Boton, clerk, his proctor, to the prebend of Wigginton in the collegiate church of Tamworth. Patron: the king. 4 December, [1418].

125.   Institution of Thomas Aleyn, chaplain, to the church of Handsworth. Patron for this turn: Edmund [Stafford], bp. of Exeter, son and heir of Richard Stafford, knt., deceased. 1 May 1419.

126.[1]   Institution of William Person, chaplain, to the vicarage of Caverswall, vacant by the resignation of John Coltan in exchange for the vicarage of Dilhorne. 7 October, [1419].

> [1] This entry breaks off in the middle, and has no reference to induction, indicating that at least one folio is missing.

127.   Institution of Thomas Conede, chaplain, to the church of Pitchford. Patron: Hugh Burnell, knt., lord of Holdgate and Weoley. Lichfield, 3 September 1416.

128.   Institution of John Walbron, chaplain, to the vicarage of Market Drayton, vacant by the resignation of Henry Falk. Patrons: P. and C. of the house of Jesus of Bethlehem near Sheen, dioc. Winchester, O.Carth. He swore obedience and continual residence. 10 December, [1416].

129.   Institution of John Duffelt ⟨sic⟩, chaplain, to the vicarage of Loppington, vacant by the resignation of Roger Ellesmer. Patrons: P. and C. of Wombridge. 11 January, [1416/17].

130.   [f.15r–v] Certificate of the vicar general to M. Geoffrey Crukadam, inceptor in both laws, canon of Salisbury cathedral, and vicar general for Robert [Hallum], bp. of Salisbury, reciting a commission from him to the vicar general of John [Catterick], bp. of Coventry and Lichfield (dated at Salisbury, under the seal of the Officiality of Salisbury, 'quod ad manus habemus', 11 March 1416/17) to inquire into a proposed exchange of benefices between John Wyndhill, rector of Cound, and John Osbarn [Osborn], rector or warden of the free chapel of Kingston Russell, dioc. Salisbury, with authority to receive Osbarn's resignation and institute Wyndhill to Kingston Russell (patron for this turn: Thomas, son of the king, duke of Clarence, earl of Aumale, and Steward of England), reserving his induction and canonical obedience. The commission had been fulfilled. Lichfield, 15 March 1416/17.

131.   [f.15v] Institution of John Osbarn, clerk, in the person of Henry Fairford, his proctor, to the rectory of Cound, vacant by the resignation offered by John Wyndehill in the hands of the vicar general for this exchange, which had been approved by him on his own authority and that of M. Geoffrey Crukeadam, inceptor in both laws and vicar general for Robert [Hallum], bp. of Salisbury. Patron: John Arundell, lord Arundel and Mautravers. 15 March, [1416/17].

132.   Institution of John Wyndhill, clerk, to the free chapel of Kingston Russell [dioc. Salisbury], by reason of the above exchange. Patron for this turn: Thomas, son of the king, duke of Clarence, earl of Aumale, and Steward of England. Same date and place as above.

133.   Institution of Richard Wyeghus, chaplain, to the rectory of Stirchley, vacant by the resignation of William Overton. Patrons: P. and C. of Wenlock. 30 June, [1416].

134.   Institution of Henry Falk, chaplain, to the vicarage of Market Drayton.

Patrons: P. and C. of the house of Jesus of Bethlehem and ⟨sic⟩ Sheen, O.Carth. He swore obedience and continual residence. 8 August, [1416].

135.   Institution of John Wyndhill, clerk, to the church of Cound. Patron for this turn:[1] the king. 17 April, [1416].

     [1] 'For this turn' interlined.

136.   Institution of M. John Hody to the church of Donington. Patrons: A. and C. of St Peter, Shrewsbury. 4 July, [1416].

137.   Institution of William Chirbury, chaplain, to the free chapel of Roding-ton. Patrons: A. and C. of St Peter, Shrewsbury. 8 April, [1416].

138.   Institution of M. William Admondeston to the wardenship of the collegiate church of St Bartholomew, Tong. Patron: Isabella, widow of Fulk de Penbrugg, knt. 18 February 1417/18.

139.   [f.16r] Institution of Richard Weston, chaplain, to the vicarage of Attingham. Patrons: A. and C. of Lilleshall. He swore obedience and continual residence. 22 February 1417/18.

140.   Institution of Thomas Wriȝt, chaplain, to the vicarage of Montford, vacant by the resignation of Richard Hamon. Patrons: Pss. and C. of white nuns, Brewood. He swore obedience and continual residence. 5 December 1418.

141.   Institution of William Felton, chaplain, to the rectory of the chapel of Ross Hall, vacant by the resignation of William Walleford. Patron: Philip Yngelfeld, lord of Ross Hall. 10 November, [1418].

142.   Institution of Edward Body, chaplain, to the chapel of Hampton. Patron: Richard Lestraunge, lord of Knockin. 8 March, [1418/19].

143.   Institution of Roger Pullurbage, chaplain, to the vicarage of Montford, vacant by the resignation of Thomas Wriȝt. Patrons: Pss. and C. of white nuns, Brewood. He swore obedience and continual residence. 9 February, [1418/19].

144.   Institution of John Don, chaplain, to the vicarage of Stanton upon Hine Heath, vacant by the resignation of Henry Falk. Patrons: A. and C. of Haugh-mond. He swore obedience and continual residence. 4 May 1419.

145.   [f.16r–v] Commission from Robert [Lancaster], bp. of St Asaph, to the bp. of Coventry and Lichfield or his vicar general to inquire into a proposed exchange of benefices between Thomas Wicherley, vicar of Baschurch, dioc. Coventry and Lichfield, and M. John Bouch, rector of Llanfachairn, dioc. St Asaph, with authority to receive John's resignation and collate Llanfachairn to Wicherley, reserving his induction and canonical obedience. He is to certify fulfilment of the commission. Monastery of Valle Crucis, dioc. St Asaph, 22 April 1419.

146. [f.16v] Note of the completion of the above exchange by the vicar general, M. John Bouch being instituted to the vicarage of Baschurch, vacant by the resignation of Thomas Wecherley in exchange for the rectory of Llanfachairn, dioc. St Asaph. He had received the resignation and investigated and approved the exchange, on his own authority and that of Robert [Lancaster], bp. of St Asaph. Patrons: A. and C. of St Peter, Shrewsbury. Bouch swore obedience and continual residence. 28 April, [1419].

147. Collation, by virtue of the above commission, of the rectory of Llanfachairn, vacant by the resignation offered by M. John Bouch in the hands of the vicar general in exchange for the vicarage of Baschurch, which he had approved, to Thomas Wicherley, chaplain. Patron: Robert [Lancaster], bp. of St Asaph. Same date and place as above.

148. Institution of John Gomond, chaplain, to the church of Berrington. Patrons: A. and C. of St Peter, Shrewsbury. 27 May, [1419].

149. Institution of Richard Wodehouse, chaplain, to the vicarage of Albrighton. Patrons: A. and C. of Dore. He swore obedience and continual residence. 14 June, [1419].

150. Institution of William Grilleshull, chaplain, to the vicarage of Wellington, vacant by the resignation of Thomas Grilleshull. Patrons: A. and C. of St Peter, Shrewsbury. He swore obedience and continual residence. 24 July, [1419].

151. [ff.16v–17r] Commission from Philip [Repingdon], bp. of Lincoln, to the bp. of Coventry and Lichfield or his vicar general, to inquire into a proposed exchange of benefices between John Bouche [Bouch], vicar of Baschurch, and John Pole, rector of a mediety of Walton, dioc. Lincoln, with authority to receive Pole's resignation and institute Bouche to the mediety of Walton (patron: Reginald de Grey, lord of Hastings, Wexford, and Ruthin). He was also to receive the oath of canonical obedience on behalf of the bishop, and issue a mandate for induction to the archdeacon of Buckingham or his Official. Sleaford Castle, 14 August 1419.

152. [f.17r] Institution of John Pole, chaplain, to the vicarage of Baschurch, vacant by the resignation offered by John Bouch in the hands of the vicar general in exchange for the mediety of the church of Walton, dioc. Lincoln, which he had approved on his own authority and that of Philip [Repingdon], bp. of Lincoln. Patrons: A. and C. of St Peter, Shrewsbury. 16 August, [1419].

153. Institution, by virtue of the above commission, of John Bouch, chaplain, to the rectory of a mediety of the church of Walton, dioc. Lincoln, vacant by the resignation offered by John Pole in the hands of the vicar general in exchange for the vicarage of Baschurch, which he had investigated, as above. Patron: Reginald de Grey, lord of Hastings, Wexford, and Ruthin. The vicar general had received his oath of canonical obedience on behalf of the bishop of Lincoln. The archdeacon of Buckingham or his Official had been mandated to induct. Same date and place as above.

[ff.17v–18v: BLANK]

154.   Institution of Thomas Killom, chaplain, to the church of Leigh. Patron: Matilda Lovell, lady Lovell and Holand. 17 April 1416.

155.   Institution of Nicholas Potter, chaplain, to the rectory of Coddington, vacant by the resignation of John Holbroke. Patrons: A. and C. of St Werburga, Chester. Lichfield, 15 May, [1416].

156.   Institution of Roger Dunvile, clerk, to a mediety of the church of Lymm. Patron: Richard de Legh, esq. 4 August, [1416].

157.   Institution of M. Philip Morgan, I.U.D., in the person of br. John Fulham, his proctor, to the church of Prescot. Patron: the king, in right of his duchy of Lancaster. 28 April 1417.

158.   Institution of M. Richard Stanley, clerk, in the person of John Iremonger, his proctor, to the church of Alderley. Patron: Robert Babthorp, knt. 27 April, [1417].

159.   Institution of Thurstan de Longley, clerk, to the church of Prestwich. Patron: Robert Longley, esq. 12 December, [1417].

160.   Institution of John Duncalf, chaplain, to the vicarage of Prestbury, vacant by the resignation of John del Shagh. Patrons: A. and C. of St Werburga, Chester. He swore obedience and continual residence. 2 March, [1417/18].

161.   Institution of Thomas Baxster, chaplain, to a chantry in Huyton church, vacant by the resignation of William de Cave. Patron: William de Assheton. He swore to observe the statutes and ordinances as used of old. 21 February 1417/18.

162.   Institution of Richard Bul, chaplain, to the church of Tattenhall, vacant by the resignation of M. John Plummer. Patrons: A. and C. of St Werburga, Chester. 18 April, [1417].

163.   [f. 19r–v] Certificate from the vicar general to John Forest, archdeacon of Surrey in Winchester cathedral, and canon of Lincoln and Lichfield cathedrals, as vicar general for Henry [Beaufort], bp. of Winchester, reciting a commission from him to John [Catterick], bp. of Coventry and Lichfield, or his vicar general (dated at St Cross, near Winchester, 14 May ⟨sic⟩ 1418) to inquire into a proposed exchange of benefices between John [de] Bradschagh, rector of Aughton, dioc. Lichfield and Coventry, and John Spynke, rector of Freshwater, dioc. Winchester, with authority to receive Spynke's resignation and admit and institute

21

Bradschagh to Freshwater (patrons: P. and C. of Sheen, O.Carth.), reserving his induction and canonical obedience. The commission had been fulfilled. Lichfield, 22 March, 1418/19.

164.   [f.19v] Institution of John Spynk, chaplain, to the church of Aughton, vacant by the resignation of John Bradschagh in exchange for the church of Freshwater, dioc. Winchester.[1] Patron: Matilda, lately wife of Roger de Bradschagh. 22 March, [1418/19].

    [1] MS: Salisbury.

165.   Institution of John Bradschagh to the church of Freshwater by reason of the above exchange. Patrons: P. and C. of Sheen. Same date and place as above.

166.   Institution of George de Radclif to the rectory of Wilmslow, vacant by the resignation of William de Bothe. Patrons: Robert de Radclif and Joan his wife. 26 July 1418.

167.   Institution of M. John Leyot, B.Dec., to the rectory of Bangor Iscoed, vacant by the resignation of John Straunge. Patron: Richard Lestraunge, knt., lord of Knockin and Ellesmere. 21 August, [1418].

168.   Institution of John Blomer, chaplain, to the church of Cheadle. Patron: Ranulf Maynwaryng. 12 August, [1418].

169.   [ff.19v–20r] Certificate to the vicar general from br. Richard [Rothley], abbot of St Mary de Pratis, Leicester, O.S.A., dioc. Lincoln, reciting a commission from the vicar general to the abbot (dated at Lichfield, 17 July, 1418, and sealed with the seal of the Officiality of the consistory of Lichfield) to inquire into a proposed exchange of benefices between Richard Frysby [Frisby], prebendary of a prebend in the collegiate church of St Mary by the Castle, Leicester, and M. Thomas Walton, prebendary of a prebend in the collegiate church of St John, Chester, with authority to receive Thomas's resignation and collate his prebend to Frysby on the bishop's authority, reserving canonical obedience, installation, and induction. The commission had been fulfilled, Frysby being admitted in the person of Richard Tamworth, his proctor. Leicester Abbey, 22 July 1418.

170.   [f.20r] Institution of Thomas Fyssheburn, chaplain, to the church of Croston. Patron for this turn: William Kenolmerssh. 4 September, [1418].

171.   Institution of Richard de Wynwyk, chaplain, to the church of Handley. Patrons: A. and C. of St Werburga, Chester. 4 September 1418.

172.   Institution of Thomas Hassale, chaplain, to the vicarage of Sandbach. Patrons: A. and C. of Dieulacres. He swore obedience and continual residence. 21 September, [1418].

173.   Institution of John Iremonger, chaplain, to the vicarage of Walton on the Hill. Patron: M. Richard Stanley, rector of Walton on the Hill. He swore obedience and continual residence. 3 October, [1418].

174.   [f.20v] Institution of Roger Spark, chaplain, to the church of Northenden. Patrons: A. and C. of St Werburga, Chester. 7 October 1418.

175.   Institution of Thomas Coppenall to the rectory of Woodchurch, vacant by the resignation of Richard Fouleshurst. Patron: Thomas de Fouleshurst, esq. 6 October, [1418].

176.   Institution of Andrew Holes, clerk, to the church of Davenham. Patron: Elizabeth, widow of Richard Vernon of Shipbrook, knt. 21 March, [1418/19].

177.   Commission from William [Barrow], bp. of Bangor, vicar general for Richard [Clifford], bp. of London, to the vicar general of John [Catterick], bp. of Coventry and Lichfield, to inquire into a proposed exchange of benefices between John Saxy, rector of a mediety of Wallasey, dioc. Coventry and Lichfield, and Edmund Tebbot, rector of Peldon, dioc. London, with authority to receive Tebbot's resignation and institute Saxy to Peldon (patrons for this turn: John Howard, Thomas Marny, and Andrew Boteler, knts., Robert Teye, William Hanyngfeld, William Clopton, John Boys, jr., and William Tendryng, esqs., and John Sumter and John Ewell), reserving induction and canonical obedience to the bp. of London or his vicar general. He is to certify fulfilment of the commission. London, sealed with the seal used in the office of vicar, 17 April 1419.

178.   [ff.20v–21r] Institution of Edmund Tebbot, chaplain, to the rectory of Wallasey, vacant by the resignation of John Saxy offered in the hands of the vicar general for this exchange, and approved by him on his own authority and that of William [Barrow], bp. of Bangor, as vicar general for Richard [Clifford], bp. of London. Patrons: A. and C. of St Werburga, Chester. 21 April, [1419].

179.   [f.21r] Institution of John Saxy to the church of Peldon, dioc. London, by reason of the above exchange. Patrons: John Howard, Thomas Marny, and Andrew Boteler, knts., Robert Teye, William Hanyngfeld, William Clopton, John Boys, jr., and William Tendryng, esqs., and John Sumter and John Ewell. Same date and place as above.

180.   Institution of William Bagelegh to the rectory of Ashton on Mersey, vacant by the resignation offered by Robert Lytster in the hands of the vicar general in exchange for the church of Wistaston, which had been approved. Patron: Richard del Assheton, esq. 30 May 1419.

181.   Institution of Robert Lytster, chaplain, in the person of Richard Spiser, his proctor, to the rectory of Wistaston, vacant by the resignation of William Baggelegh offered in the hands of the vicar general in exchange for the church of Ashton [on Mersey], which had been approved. Patrons: John Bresty and Hugh del Malpas, esqs. Same date and place as above.

182.   Institution of George de Raddecliff, chaplain, to the church of Wilmslow, vacant by the failure of the recovery of Geoffrey Boseley, clerk, in the king's court at Chester. Patron: Robert del Bothe, esq. 11 September, [1419].

183.　　Royal writ to the bishop notifying him that Robert del Bothe had recovered the presentation to Wilmslow church against Geoffrey de Boseley, clerk, before the royal justices at Chester, and ordering the admission of a suitable person presented by him. Attested by James del Holt, justice of Chester. Chester, 15 May, 7 Henry V [1419].

184.　　Royal writ to the bishop to execute the above writ, or certify why he will not or cannot do so. Attested by James del Holt, justice of Chester. Chester, 4 September, 7 Henry V [1419].

185.　　[f.21v] Formal record of the oath of obedience to the bishop offered by br. Thomas ʒerdeley [ʒerdley], abbot of St Werburga, Chester. In the presence of M. Thomas Barton, treasurer of Lichfield, M. Walter Bullok, M. William Newhagh, and Walter Piers, canons of Lichfield, M. William Forbour, M. Robert Duffeld, and M. John Barbour, notaries public, and others. The notaries were asked to draw up a public instrument. Lichfield cathedral, chapel of St Mary, 28 July 1419.

[f.22r: BLANK]

186.　　[f.22v] Dispensation granted to permit the marriage between William le Massy, son of Hamo le Massy, and Petronilla, daughter of Richard de Werburton, in accordance with a recited commission of Jordan [Orsini], bp. of Albano and papal penitentiary (and dated at Constance, 5 ides January, 5 John XXIII [9 January 1414/15]), notwithstanding their relationship in the fourth degree of consanguinity on both sides. Sealed with the seal of the Officiality of the consistory of Lichfield. Lichfield, 10 August 1415.

REGISTRUM DISPENSATIONUM SUPER DEFECTIBUS NATALIUM, CONTRAC-
TUUM MATRIMONIALIUM A IURE PROHIBITORUM, CELEBRATIONUM ORDINUM, AC
ALIARUM DIVERSARUM EXECUCIONUM FACTARUM ET CONCESSARUM PER VENER-
ABILEM VIRUM MAGISTRUM WALTERUM BULLOK, IN LEGIBUS LICENTIATI ⟨sic⟩,
ECCLESIE CATHEDRALE LICHFELDENSIS CANONICI⟨sic⟩, REVERENDI IN CHRISTO
PATRIS ET DOMINI, DOMINI JOHANNIS, DEI GRATIA COVENTRENSIS ET LICHFEL-
DENSIS EPISCOPI, IPSO IN REMOTIS AGENTE, VICARII ⟨sic⟩ IN SPIRITUALIBUS GENER-
ALIS, ANNO DOMINI MILLESIMO CCCCmo QUINTODECIMO.

187.[1]   Marginal note that the dispensation for the marriage between William
le Ma[ssy] and Petronilla, daughter of [Richard de] Werburton, which should be
entered here, is on the facing folio [no. 186, f. 22v].
    [1] The margin is here damaged, the parts of words in [] being supplied to cover
    the damaged portions.

188.   Dispensation from irregularity granted to John Loghtborowe [Loghte-
borowe, Loughtebourgh], canon of Charley, in accordance with a recited commission to the bp. of Lichfield or his vicar general from Jordan [Orsini], bishop of
Albano and penitentiary of the apostolic see (dated at Constance, 12 kal. July [20
June], 1415).
    The petitioner, a priest and professed canon of Charley, O.S.A., dioc.
Lincoln, had claimed that a certain br. Robert, prior of the monastery, fearing
deposition from office by the founder on account of his bad rule and unfit life, had
been falsely informed that the petitioner had been trying to procure this by
contacts with the founder and others, and had for several days displayed anger
towards the petitioner. When the petitioner knew of the cause, he protested and
demonstrated his innocence to the prior. One day thereafter the petitioner sought
licence from the prior to go and work in the monastery meadow, which being
granted he took with him two of the *famuli* (one aged 80, the other 12 or
thereabouts). After a short time the prior followed with two kinsmen, each
carrying a fork with iron points, and started to argue with the petitioner that his
work was not good and he was inept at haymaking. The petitioner suffered this
patiently, but the prior became increasingly angry, and unable to contain himself
suddenly struck the petitioner on the head with one of the forks, rendering him
stupefied. The prior, overcome by anger, gave another blow, and blood from the
wound flowed over the petitioner's face, and he fell to the ground as though dead.
The prior then incited his kinsmen to finish him off, and one gave him a third
cruel blow with a wooden implement. The eighty-year-old then exhorted the
petitioner to get up, otherwise he would be killed. He recovered, seeing the prior
wishing to pin him to the ground with the fork through his chest, but he got him
through the arm instead. The prior's kinsmen had meanwhile been prevented
from attacking the petitioner by certain men and women who were haymaking in
the field. The prior, wishing to finish off what he had started, pushed the
petitioner backwards with the fork (which was still stuck in him so that he could

not extricate himself), until he would fall over a heap of hay and again fall supine so that the prior would be able to kill him. The petitioner, realising what would happen, reached out to grab the arm of a bystander to support himself. Contrary to Loghtborowe's intention the bystander drew out a knife, thinking that he intended to defend himself (although the petitioner did not know whose knife it was, being so covered with blood that he could not see). He was highly fearful, the prior being stronger than he was; there being the pile of hay behind him which (if he fell on it) would mean his death; there was nowhere to flee to at the sides; and he knew that there were three enemies who could run faster than he. He pleaded with the prior to stop, but the prior declared that he intended to kill him. The petitioner, then realising that there was no other way to evade death, stuck the knife in the prior's chest, although without being aware of where he had struck him because he was blinded by blood; and the prior fell to the ground and shortly afterwards died, although before that publicly confessed that he had intended to kill the petitioner, who had only stabbed him in self-defence. In the circumstances, Loghtborowe sought remedy from the apostolic see, and the commission had been sent to the vicar general because the petitioner did not dare to approach his own ordinary. The investigation found that he was not to blame for the death, having acted in self-defence to save his life. He had therefore incurred no excommunication or irregularity. Lichfield, 4 September 1415.

189.   [f.24r] Dispensation granted to permit the marriage between Thomas, son of John de Assheton, knt., and Elizabeth, daughter of John de Buron,[1] knt., in accordance with a recited commission from Jordan [Orsini], bp. of Albano and penitentiary of the vacant apostolic see, to the bp. of Lichfield or his vicar general (dated at Constance, 3 ides [11] December, 1416), and notwithstanding the impediment that Thomas, when aged 11, had consented to a marriage with Alice, sister of Elizabeth, who had died at the age of 8. Lichfield, sealed with the seal of the Officiality of the consistory of Lichfield, 17 April 1417.

> [1] The margin gives the surname as Burton.

190.   [f.24r–v] Dispensation granted to Robert Sonke, scholar, in accordance with a recited commission from Jordan [Orsini], bp. of Albano and penitentiary of the vacant apostolic see, to the bp. of Coventry and Lichfield or his vicar general (dated at Constance, 19 kal. September [14 August], 1417), allowing him to acquire clerical status, receive orders, and acquire a benefice, notwithstanding that he was the son of a single man and a single woman. If he obtains a benefice, he is to take orders in due time, and reside in person. Lichfield, 14 November 1418.

191.[1]   [f.24v] Dispensation granted to William Smyth, clerk,[2] in accordance with a recited commission from Jordan [Orsini], bp. of Albano and penitentiary of the vacant apostolic see, to the bp. of Lichfield or his vicar general (dated at Constance, 4 kal. February [29 January], 1416/17), allowing him to receive orders and acquire a benefice, notwithstanding that he was the son of a priest and a single

> [1] This entry is incomplete: it breaks off in mid-sentence, and lacks a dating clause, indicating that at least one leaf is missing here.
> [2] He is called an acolyte in the commission.

woman. If he obtains a benefice, he is to take orders in due time, and reside in person.

192.　　[f.25r] Dispensation granted to Ralph, son of Ralph de Radeclif, knt., and Cecilia, daughter of the late Robert Graven [Graver], knt., in accordance with a recited commission from Jordan [Orsini], bp. of Albano and penitentiary of the vacant apostolic see, to the bp. of Coventry and Lichfield or his vicar general (dated at Constance, 19 kal. September [14 August], 1416). They had petitioned for the dispensation to allow them to remain married, having gone through a form of marriage whilst aware of the impediment caused by the double relationship in the fourth degree of consanguinity between Ralph and Hugh [de] Venables, who had been Cecilia's first husband. They were to be absolved from their excommunication, have penance imposed, and the survivor of their marriage was to remain unmarried thereafter. They may contract marriage anew. Lichfield, 25 October 1418.

193.　　[f.25v] Dispensation granted to permit the marriage between William, son of John [de] Butterworth,[1] and Isabella, daughter of Bucley,[2] in accordance with a recited commission from Jordan [Orsini], bp. of Albano and penitentiary of the vacant apostolic see, to the bp. of Lichfield or his vicar general (dated at Constance, 7 ides [7] December, 1416), notwithstanding the impediment of their relationship in the third and third degrees of affinity. Lichfield, 6 February, [1417/18].[3]

　　[1] The marginal title gives the surname as Butterley.
　　[2] The marginal title gives the surname as Bulcley. There is no indication of her father's Christian name.
　　[3] See also below, no. 197.

194.　　[ff.25v–26r] Dispensation granted to John Hatton and Margaret, daughter of John Hycheson[1] of Sankey, in accordance with a recited commission from Jordan [Orsini], bp. of Albano and papal penitentiary, to the bp. of Lichfield or his vicar general (dated at Constance, 8 ides May, 5 John XXIII [8 May, 1415]). They had petitioned for the confirmation of their marriage, contracted in ignorance of the impediment of affinity caused by the earlier fornication between John and a certain Alice, who was related to Margaret in the fourth degree of consanguinity, and which was not revealed before the solemnisation and confirmation of the marriage. The investigation revealed that although unaware of the impediment at the contracting and consummation of the marriage, they did know of it prior to the solemnisation. Lichfield, sealed with the seal of the Officiality of the consistory of Lichfield, 6 September 1419.

　　[1] The marginal title gives the surname as Hychonson.

195.　　[f.26r] Note of a dispensation granted to Thomas Leyot,[1] scholar, the son of a priest and a single woman, in accordance with a commission from Jordan [Orsini], bp. of Albano and papal penitentiary, allowing him to receive orders and acquire a benefice. If he obtains a benefice, he is to take orders in due time, and

　　[1] The marginal title gives the surname as Layot.

27

reside in person. Testimonial letters had been issued under the seal of the Officiality of Lichfield. Lichfield, 28 April 1417.

196.   Note of a dispensation granted to David de Oreton, scholar, son of a single man and a single woman, in accordance with a commission from Jordan [Orsini], bp. of Albano and penitentiary of the vacant apostolic see, allowing him to receive orders and acquire a benefice. If he obtains a benefice, he is to take orders in due time, and reside in person. Testimonial letters had been issued under the seal of the Officiality of Lichfield. 9 March, [1417/18].

197.   [f.26r–v] Repeat of no. 193 (with surnames in the addressing clause spelt Butturworth, Bulkeley), the report of the investigation referring to an impediment of consanguinity (although the commission, as in 193, refers to affinity), and with new date of 12 March 1417/18.

198.   [f.26v] Dispensation granted to John Molyngton, clerk, in accordance with a recited commission from Jordan [Orsini], bp. of Albano and penitentiary of the vacant apostolic see, to the bp. of Lichfield or his vicar general (dated at Constance, 4 nones [4] October, 1416), allowing him to receive orders and acquire a benefice, notwithstanding that he was the son of a priest and a single woman, and had concealed the impediment when acquiring a clerical character, which he wishes to retain. He was absolved, and a suitable penance imposed. If he obtains a benefice, he is to take orders in due time, and reside in person. Lichfield, sealed with the seal of the Officiality of Lichfield, 12 March 1417/18.

199.   [f.27r] Dispensation from irregularity[1] granted to John Holand, chaplain,[2] in accordance with a recited commission from Jordan [Orsini], bp. of Albano and penitentiary of the vacant apostolic see, to the bp. of Lichfield or his vicar general (dated at Constance, 2 nones [14] October 1416). The petitioner had clandestinely married John Philippi of Egerton and Margaret Johannis Waryn, without licence from their curate, and had thereby incurred excommunication. In his ignorance, he had continued to celebrate offices and minister, and now sought remedy. He was temporarily suspended from his priestly functions. Lichfield, sealed with the seal of the Officiality of the consistory of Lichfield, 12 April 1417.

[1] The marginal title mistakenly records this as a matrimonial dispensation for the couple whose marriage had been clandestinely celebrated.
[2] He is called a priest in the commission.

200.   [f.27r–v] General notification of the deliverance of Alan Rider, chaplain. He had been indicted before the royal justices at Stafford on accusations that on the Wednesday in Whit week, 10 Henry IV [29 May, 1409], he had broken into Standon church and stolen two books worth 6 marks belonging to that church, and was a common thief, highwayman, and despoiler of fields; that on Maundy Thursday, 10 Henry IV [4 April, 1409], he had broken into the house and chamber of Roger Porter of Cresswell and had stolen 21s. 8d. in cash; that on the Saturday before the Nativity of St John the Baptist, 10 Henry IV [22 June 1409], he had broken into the house of William Mathewe at Cresswell, and stolen 20s.

8d. in cash; and that on the same date he had stolen 4 lbs. of wool worth 18d. and 20d. in cash from Adam Ladyman at Cresswell, and a pair of cloths price 4s. from Juliane Tailour. He had been imprisoned as a convicted clerk in the bishop's prison for some time, and sought purgation. After due proclamation according to the law he had appeared before the vicar general in the prebendal church of Eccleshall on the Saturday after Trinity [17 June] 1419. No objectors had appeared, and he had purged himself by the oath of sufficient clerks. Lichfield, sealed with the seal of the Officiality of the consistory of Lichfield, 30 June 1419.

201.   [f.27v] General notification of the deliverance of John Burton of Copeland, Lancs. He had been indicted (as a labourer) before the royal justices at Chester on the charge that, on Thursday, the feast of the Purification of the Blessed Virgin Mary, 6 Henry V [2 February 1418/19], he had stolen a strip of silver fixed to the right foot of the image of the Holy Trinity in the church of Holy Trinity, Chester, worth 6s. 8d., but was denounced, captured by the king's ministers, and imprisoned. At the court held by the mayor and sheriff of that city on the Monday before the feast of St Valentine, 6 Henry V [13 February 1418/19], the archdeacon of Chester claimed him for the ecclesiastical courts in accordance with the customs of the city. He had been imprisoned in the bishop's prison as a convicted clerk, and had sought purgation. After due proclamation according to law he had appeared before John Norton, vicar of the prebendal church of Eccleshall, and commissary of the vicar general for this matter, in the prebendal church of Eccleshall, on 10 July 1419. No objectors had appeared, and he had purged himself by the oath of sufficient clerks. Lichfield, 12 July 1419.

202.   [ff.27v–28v] Dispensation granted to Thurstan de Pemburton and Emmote de Wynstanley,[1] in accordance with two recited commissions from Jordan [Orsini], bp. of Albano and penitentiary of the vacant apostolic see, to the bp. of Lichfield or his vicar general, both dated at Constance, 2 nones [4] February, 1416/17. The first sets out their petition, that they had married clandestinely, although aware of the impediment of affinity arising from the previous fornication between Thurstan and Cecilia de le Mesch, who was doubly related to Emmote in the third degree of consanguinity. They had lived together as man and wife, and had children, but when the marriage had been brought to the attention of the ordinary, he had investigated, and ordered their separation. They wished to recontract their marriage. They were to be absolved from their excommunication, have penance imposed, and the survivor of their marriage was to remain unmarried thereafter. The children were to be legitimised. The second commission repeats the terms of the first, stating that the marriage had been contracted although they were aware of the impediment of their relationship in the fourth and fourth degrees of consanguinity. The vicar general's investigation had confirmed the relationship set out in the first commission,[2] and the marriage had been confirmed. Sealed with the seal of the Officiality of the consistory of Lichfield, 6 June 1417.

[1]   The marginal title mistakenly describes this as a matrimonial dispensation for Pemburton and Cecilia de le Mesch. In the commissions, Pemburton and Wynstanley are described as noble *domicelli*.
[2]   No mention is made in the dispensing clause of the facts alleged in the second commission from the penitentiary.

203.　　Dispensation to permit the marriage between Thurstan [de] Halle and Denise Eyre,[1] in accordance with a recited commission from Jordan [Orsini], bp. of Albano, penitentiary of the vacant apostolic see, to the bp. of Lichfield or his vicar general (dated at Constance, 16 kal. April 1417 [17 March 1417/18]), notwithstanding the impediment of their relationship in the fourth degree of consanguinity. Lichfield, 6 July 1419.

　　　　[1] The marginal title gives the surname as Eyer.

204.　　[ff.28v–29v] Dispensation for Ralph de Langtre and Isabella Levelerd [Leverlord], in accordance with two recited commissions from Jordan [Orsini], bp. of Albano and penitentiary of the vacant apostolic see, to the bp. of Lichfield or his vicar general. The first (dated at Constance, 3 nones [3] February 1416/17), requires him to investigate their petition for a dispensation, setting out that they wished to marry, notwithstanding the impediment of their relationship in the fourth degree of consanguinity. The second (dated at Constance, nones [5] February 1416/17) refers to the above, which the petitioners feared might be invalid, as one party was related to the other in the third rather than fourth degree of consanguinity, and they had sought a remedy. Pope Clement VI in similar cases had declared that such grants would be effective notwithstanding the omission of the mention of the third degree, and the previous commission is confirmed. The vicar general's investigation had revealed that Ralph was related to Isabella in the third degree, and she to him in the fourth. Lichfield, sealed with the seal of the Officiality of the consistory of Lichfield, 4 August 1417.

205.　　[f.29v] Note of a dispensation granted in accordance with letters from Anthony [da Ponte], bp. of Concordia, penitentiary in the absence of Jordan [Orsini], bp. of Albano and chief papal penitentiary, to Richard Venables, scholar, son of a single man and a single woman, allowing him to receive orders and acquire a benefice. If he obtains a benefice he is to take orders in due time and reside in person. Testimonial letters had been issued under the seal of the Officiality of the consistory of Lichfield. Lichfield, 20 December 1418.

206.　　Note of a dispensation granted in accordance with letters from Anthony [da Ponte], bp. of Concordia, penitentiary in the absence of Jordan [Orsini], bp. of Albano and chief papal penitentiary, to William Venables, scholar, son of a single man and a single woman, allowing him to receive orders and acquire a benefice. If he obtains a benefice he is to take orders in due time, and reside in person. Testimonial letters had been issued, sealed as above. Lichfield, 20 December, [1418].

207.　　Note of a dispensation granted in accordance with similar letters, to Peter de Venables, scholar, son of a single man and a single woman, allowing him to receive orders and acquire a benefice. If he obtains a benefice he is to take orders in due time, and reside in person. Testimonial letters had been issued, sealed as above. Lichfield, 20 December, [1418].

208.　　Note of a dispensation granted in accordance with similar letters, to John Venables, scholar, son of a single man and a single woman, allowing him to receive orders and acquire a benefice. If he obtains a benefice he is to take orders in due time and reside in person. Testimonial letters had been issued, sealed as above. Lichfield, 20 December, [1418].

209.   [ff.29v–30r] General notification, addressed especially to Thomas Grillushull, formerly perpetual vicar of the prebendal church of Wellington, and William[1] Grillushull, now vicar of that church, setting out the ordination of a pension from the vicarage. Thomas and William in person, and the abbot and convent of St Peter, Shrewsbury, the patrons of the vicarage, by letters patent under their seal, had agreed to be bound by the vicar-general's ordination of a life pension for Thomas, payable by William and his successors, they two agreeing by corporal oath taken on the gospels. After an inquisition into the true value of the vicarage, the pension was ordained as follows: £10 per year, payable in equal parts at Easter and Michaelmas in Wellington church, for food and clothing; Thomas is to have a chamber and fireplace on the east side of the hall, with free entry and exit within the vicarage of Wellington. A threefold and peremptory monition was issued to the present and future vicars for payment at or within twenty days of the said terms, on pain of major excommunication for themselves, interdict on the vicarage, and sequestration of income. William took an oath to make payment. Future vicars are to take an oath on their admission. The bishop reserves the right as diocesan superior for himself and his successors to compel payment by other ecclesiastical censures and legal remedies. Sealed with the seal of the Officiality of the consistory of Lichfield, 22 July 1419.

    [1] At one point he is mistakenly named John.

210.   [f.30r–v] Dispensation granted to John Savage, clerk, in accordance with a recited commission from Jordan [Orsini], bp. of Albano, penitentiary of the vacant apostolic see, to the bp. of Lichfield or his vicar general (dated at Constance, ides [13] June 1417), allowing him to receive orders and acquire a benefice, notwithstanding that he was the son of a single man and a single woman. If he obtains a benefice, he is to take orders in due time, and reside in person. Lichfield, 18 February 1417/18.

211.   [ff.30v–31r] Dispensation granted to William Inse, clerk,[1] in accordance with a recited commission from Jordan [Orsini], bp. of Albano and papal penitentiary, to the bp. of Lichfield or his vicar general (dated at Constance, 3 ides January, 5 John XXIII [11 January 1414/15]), allowing him to acquire a clerical character, receive orders, and acquire a benefice, notwithstanding that he was the son of a priest and a single woman. If he obtains a benefice, he is to take orders in due time, and reside in person. Lichfield, sealed with the seal of the Officiality of the consistory of Lichfield, 12 January 1417/18.

    [1] Described as a scholar in the commission.

212.   [f.31r] Dispensation granted to Richard Madak,[1] scholar, in accordance with a recited commission from Anthony [da Ponte], bp. of Concordia, penitentiary in the absence of Jordan [Orsini], bp. of Albano and chief papal penitentiary,

    [1] The (later) marginal title gives the name as William Maddocks.

31

to the bp. of Lichfield or his vicar general (sealed with the seal of the chief penitentiary, and dated at Geneva, 12 kal. July, 1 Martin V [20 June 1418]), allowing him to acquire a clerical character, receive orders, and acquire a benefice, notwithstanding that he was the son of a single man and a single woman, who were related in the third degree of consanguinity. If he obtains a benefice, he is to take orders in due time, and reside in person. Lichfield, 16 December 1418.

213.   [f.31r–v] Dispensation granted to Robert Lawnlyn [Lawncelyn], scholar, in accordance with a recited commission from Anthony [da Ponte], bp. of Concordia, acting papal penitentiary in the absence of Jordan [Orsini], bp. of Albano, chief papal penitentiary, to the bp. of Lichfield or his vicar general (sealed with the seal of the chief penitentiary, and dated at Geneva, 6 kal. July, 1 Martin V [26 June 1418]), allowing him to acquire a clerical character, receive orders, and acquire a benefice, notwithstanding that he was the son of a single man and a single woman. If he obtains a benefice, he is to take orders in due time, and reside in person. Lichfield, 12 September 1418.

214.   [f.31v] Note of a dispensation granted in accordance with letters of Anthony [da Ponte], bp. of Concordia, penitentiary in the absence of Jordan [Orsini], bp. of Albano and chief papal penitentiary, to Hugh Penynton, scholar, son of a single man and a single woman, allowing him to receive orders and acquire a benefice. If he obtains a benefice he is to take orders in due time, and reside in person. Testimonial letters had been issued under the seal of the Officiality of the consistory of Lichfield. Lichfield, 20 September 1418.

215.   [ff.31v–32r] Notarial instrument, drawn up at the request of the vicar general, and sealed with the seal of the Officiality of the consistory of Lichfield, recording a dispensation granted to Hugh Fytton, clerk,[1] in accordance with a recited commission from Anthony [da Ponte], bp. of Concordia, penitentiary in the absence of Jordan [Orsini], bp. of Albano and chief papal penitentiary, to the bp. of Lichfield or his vicar general (sealed with the seal of the chief penitentiary and dated at Mantua, 5 kal. January, 2 Martin V [28 December 1418]), allowing him to acquire a clerical character, receive orders, and acquire a benefice, notwithstanding that he was the son of a single man and a single woman. If he obtains a benefice, he is to take orders in due time and reside in person. In the presence of M. John Fytton, archdeacon of Stafford, and M. Robert Duffeld, notary public, and others. Attestation by John Barbour, clerk, dioc. Coventry and Lichfield, notary public. Lichfield cathedral, 18 February 1418/19.

  [1] Described as a scholar in the commission.

216.   [f.32r–v] Dispensation granted to William Clayton, clerk,[1] in accordance with a recited commission from Jordan [Orsini], bp. of Albano and papal penitentiary, to the bp. of Lichfield or his vicar general (dated at Florence, 10 kal. April, 2 Martin V [23 March 1418/19]). He was the son of a single man and a single woman, but had concealed the impediment when obtaining minor orders. He wished to retain and minister in those orders, receive further orders, and

  [1] Described as an acolyte in the commission.

acquire a benefice. He is to be absolved from his excommunication and have suitable penance imposed. If he obtains a benefice, he is to take orders in due time and reside in person. Lichfield, sealed with the seal of the Officiality of the consistory of Lichfield, 12 June 1419.

217.	[f.32v] Notarial instrument, drawn up at the request of the vicar general, and sealed with the seal of the Officiality of Lichfield, recording a dispensation to permit the marriage of Ranulf, alias Houkyn, de Chernok, and Alice de Radclyf [Radeclyf], granted in accordance with a recited commission from Anthony [da Ponte], bp. of Concordia, penitentiary in the absence of Jordan [Orsini], bp. of Albano and chief papal penitentiary, to the bp. of Lichfield or his vicar general (sealed with the seal of the chief penitentiary, and dated at Mantua, 5 kal. February, 2 Martin V [28 January 1418/19]), and notwithstanding the impediment of their relationship in the fourth degree of consanguinity. In the presence of Robert Stronge, chaplain, Henry Fayrford, litteratus, Robert, and others. Attestation by John Barbour, clerk, dioc. Coventry and Lichfield, notary public. Lichfield cathedral, 5 October 1419.

218.	[f.33r] General notification by Thomas de Stretton, dean, and the chapter of Lichfield cathedral, of their admission of M. Maior Parys to the canonry and prebend of Bobenhull in that cathedral, reciting a commission from the vicar general (dated at Lichfield, 12 December 1417, and sealed with the seal of the Officiality of the consistory of Lichfield), setting out that the canonry was vacant by the resignation of M. William Goldeston, and had been collated to Parys. They were to admit and install him or his proctor to the stall in choir and place in chapter associated with the prebend, and certify their actions. The commission had been fulfilled, Parys being personally admitted as canon and installed and given his place in chapter on 8 February 1417/18, after taking an oath to observe the statutes and customs of the church and of canonical obedience. Chapter house, Lichfield, for sealing ('quo ad consignacionem presencium'), 28 February 1417/18.

[ff.33v–34v: BLANK]

219.   Ordination held by John [Stockes], bp. of Kilmore, in Lichfield cathedral, 21 September 1415, by licence from John [Catterick], bp. of Coventry and Lichfield.

Acolytes

Matthew Kelcheth
John Stephene

Secular subdeacons

Henry Whitesith, by l.d., to t. Repton
Thomas Hewlot, by l.d., to t. Henwood
Robert Hosier, by l.d., to t. Canons Ashby
Thomas Shyngler, by l.d., to t. Burton

Secular deacons

Roger Ardeweke, to t. Burscough
William Clerc, by l.d., to t. Hailes
William London, by l.d., to t. Wombridge
Thomas Siryth, by l.d., to t. Ranton
Roger Goodman, by l.d., to t. Ranton
Edward Warde, to t. St James, Bridgnorth
Robert Bowland, to t. Upholland
Richard Walton, to t. Burscough
Gilbert Sonky, to t. Vale Royal
John Koc, to t. Haughmond
William Dawes, to t. St Giles, Shrewsbury
John Busch, to t. Lilleshall

Secular priests

John Bewford, dioc. Lichfield, to t. collegiate church of St Mary, Southwell
Robert Blakelowe, to t. Whalley
Ralph Baxster, to t. Hulton
Robert Corker, to t. Burscough
Robert Harden, to t. Shelford
William Grossefeld, to t. St Katherine, Lincoln
Richard Russheton, to t. St James, Bridgnorth
John Wolaston, to t. Ranton
Richard Spicer of Foxton, dioc. Lincoln, by l.d., to t. St John, Leicester
[col. b] Richard Warde, by l.d., to t. Hailes
William Wordworth, by l.d. to t. Monk Bretton

¹ Unless otherwise stated, the ordaining bishop was throughout acting on commission from the vicar general.

Religious subdeacons

br. Thomas Rugeley, canon of Arbury
br. Richard Gloucestre, canon of Arbury
br. Richard Shiplond, canon of Arbury
br. Thomas More, monk of Burton
br. Nicholas Warde, monk of Burton
br. Thomas Norton, monk of Burton
br. Henry Asshebourne, monk of Burton
br. Richard Burnell, canon of Haughmond
br. John Aston, monk of Shrewsbury

Religious deacons

br. John Milde, O.P., of Shrewsbury convent
br. Roger Leton, canon of Haughmond

Religious priests

br. Richard Swepston, O.P., of Leicester
br. Louis Rideley, O.P., of Shrewsbury convent
br. John Atherston, monk of Merevale
br. Robert Preston, monk of Merevale
br. Adam Broghton, canon of Baswich

220.   [f.35r–v] Ordination held by Simon [Brampton], bp. *Tripolitanensis*. 20 December 1415.

Acolytes

William Wright
James Travell
Thomas Thake
Richard Ricard

Thomas Wethenale
John Wymark
John Westley

Secular subdeacons

John Kirkcorme, by l.d., to t. Burscough
Richard Kefex, to t. Trentham
William Fissher, to t. Repton
Richard Twenbrokus, to t. Rocester
William Stanley, dioc. York, by l.d., to t. Shelford
[f.35v] Gilbert de Hesketh, by l.d., to t. Upholland
Thomas atte Wer, to t. St John, Coventry

Secular deacons

Henry Whitesith, to t. Repton
Robert Hosier, dioc. Lincoln, by l.d., to t. Canons Ashby
Thomas Hewlot, by l.d., to t. Henwood
Thomas Shyngler, to t. Burton

Secular priests

William Clerk, to t. Hailes
Roger Ardeweke, to t. Burscough
Edward Wade, to t. St J[ames], Bridgnorth
John Koc, to t. Haughmond
Robert Bowlond, to t. Upholland
Gilbert Sonky, to t. Vale Royal
Richard Walton, to t. Burscough

Religious subdeacons

br. John Morton, canon of Baswich

Religious deacons

br. Thomas More, monk of Burton
br. Nicholas Warde, monk of Burton
br. Thomas Norton, monk of Burton
br. Henry Asshebourne, monk of Burton

221.   [f.35v] Ordination held in Lichfield cathedral by Simon [Brampton], bp. *Tripolitanensis*. 13 March 1415/16.

Acolytes

Michael Kirkeby
William Hunte
John Bruyne
John Ade
John Hichons
John Wodehouse
Laurence Hatton

Robert Childe
John Verney
Giles Asteley
John Broun
John Gibbons
Ralph Stanley
Henry Clerc

Secular subdeacons

William Brome, to t. Beauchief
Thomas Bertem, to t. Dale
Roger Bowher, to t. Dale
[col. b] Thomas Kyrkeby, to t. Dale
Roger Baker, to t. nuns of St Mary, Chester
Richard Beuglegh, to t. Vale Royal
Thomas Scaunsby, to t. Darley
Philip Jeykyn, to t. Lilleshall
John Wymark, to t. Baswich
Edward Rede, to t. St Giles, Shrewsbury
John Hatton, to t. Wombridge
John Pach, to t. Hailes
William Wryght, dioc. York, by l.d., to t. nuns of St Clement, York

Secular deacons

Thomas atte Were, to t. St John, Coventry
Nicholas Hyll, to t. Dale

Richard Kefex, to t. Trentham
John Kirkcorme, to t. Burscough
Gilbert Hesketh, to t. Upholland
William Fissher, to t. Repton
William Stanley, dioc. York, by l.d., to t. Shelford
Richard Twenbrokus, to t. Rocester

Secular priests

Henry Whitesith, to t. Repton
William Dawes, to t. St Giles, Shrewsbury
Thomas Hewlot, to t. Henwood
Robert Hosier, dioc. Lincoln, by l.d., to t. Canons Ashby

Religious acolytes

br. Bartholomew Holkote
br. John Burton, canon of Church Gresley
br. Richard Colman, canon of Baswich

Religious subdeacons

br. John Arnall
br. Maurice Pole
br. John Bredon, canon of Church Gresley
br. Robert Melbourne, canon of Church Gresley

Religious deacons

br. John Morton, canon of Baswich

Religious priests

br. John Marley

222. [f.36r] Ordination held in Lichfield cathedral by Simon [Brampton],
bp. *Tripolitanensis*. 4 April 1416.

Acolytes

Reginald de Tarlton
Thomas Fraunceys

Secular subdeacons

John Verney, rector of the free chapels of Cuckow Church and Wadborough,
    dioc. Worcester.
James Travell, by l.d., to t. hospital of St John[2] near Stafford
John Gybon, to t. Tutbury
Ranulf Stanley, to t. Birkenhead
Laurence de Hatton, to t. Whalley
William Honte, to t. Church Gresley
John Westley, to t. hospital of St John, Coventry

    [2] MS: James

37

Henry Clerk, to t. Burton

Secular deacons

William Brome, to t. Beauchief
Thomas Bertrem, to t. Dale
Roger Baker, to t. nuns of St Mary, Chester
William Wryght, dioc. York, by l.d., to t. nuns of St Clement near York
Thomas Scaumsby, to t. Darley
Edward Rede, to t. hospital of St Giles, Shrewsbury
John Wymark, to t. Baswich
Philip Jeykyn, to t. Lilleshall
Richard Beuglegh, to t. Vale Royal
Thomas Swynburn, dioc. Durham, by l.d., to t. nuns of St Mary, Sulby

Secular priests

Thomas atte Wer, to t. St John, Coventry
Richard Kefex, to t. Trentham
William Stanley, dioc. York, by l.d., to t. Shelford
Gilbert Hesketh, to t. Upholland

[col. b] Religious acolytes

br. John Holt, O.F.M., from Lichfield convent

Religious subdeacons

br. John Burton, canon of Church Gresley

Religious deacons

br. Maurice Pole, O.F.M., from Lichfield convent
br. John Bredon, canon of Church Gresley
br. Robert Melbourne, canon of Church Gresley

Religious priests

br. William Worsop, monk of Stoneleigh

223.   Ordination held in the chapel of St Mary in the Square, Lichfield, by S[imon Brampton], bp. *Tripolitanensis*. 18 April 1416.

Subdeacons

Matthew de Kelcheth, by l.d., to t. Burscough

Deacons

John Verney, rector of the free chapels of Cuckow Church and Wadborough, dioc. Worcester
James Travell, to t. hospital of St John near Stafford

Religious deacons

br. John Burton, canon of Church Gresley

224.   Ordination held in Lichfield cathedral by S[imon Brampton], bp. *Tripolitanensis*. 13 June 1416.

Acolytes

Thurstan Longley, rector of Prestwich, by l.d.
John Bonyngton   Roger Clerk
John Nowell   John Bradwell, rector of Birdingbury
John Newman
John Offeley

Secular subdeacons

Roger Dunvyle, rector of a mediety of Lymm
[f. 36v] William Boseworth, to t. Repton
John Ady, to t. Wombridge
John Smethurst, to t. Whalley
Reginald Tarlton, to t. Burscough
Robert Chylde, dioc. Lincoln, by l.d., to t. Pipewell
Thomas Widenale, dioc. Lincoln, by l.d., to t. Sulby
Henry Sutton, to t. Burscough

Secular deacons

William Honte, to t. Church Gresley
John Gybon, to t. Tutbury
John Westley, to t. hospital of St John, Coventry
John Pach, to t. Hailes
Henry Clerk, to t. Burton on Trent
Ranulf Stanley, to t. Birkenhead
Laurence de Hatton, to t. Whalley
John Hatton, to t. Wombridge

Secular priests

Thomas Scaumsby, to t. Darley
Philip Jeykyn, to t. Lilleshall
Edward Rede, to t. hospital of St Giles, Shrewsbury
William Fissher, to t. Repton
William Wright, dioc. York, by l.d., to t. nuns of St Clement near York
William Brome, to t. Beauchief
John Wymark, to t. Baswich
Roger Baker, to t. nuns of St Mary, Chester
Thomas Bertrem, to t. Dale
John Kirkorme, to t. Burscough
James Travell, to t. hospital of St John near Stafford
Robert Twenbrokus, to t. Rocester
Thomas Schyngler, to t. Burton
John Verney, rector of the free chapels of Cuckow Church and Wadborough,
    dioc. Worcester

Religious acolytes

br. Alexander Aldelem, canon of Trentham

Religious subdeacons

br. Hugh Lawe, monk of Vale Royal
br. Ralph Clydirowe, monk of Whalley
br. Thomas de Harden, monk of Whalley
br. Roger de Nonnwyk, monk of Whalley
[col. b] br. Thomas London, monk of Coventry
br. Thomas Pollesworth, monk of Coventry
br. John Northampton, monk of Coventry
br. John Grene, canon of Maxstoke

Religious deacons

br. John Abyndon, O.Carm, of Coventry
br. John Newson, O.Carm., of Coventry
br. John Aston, monk of Shrewsbury
br. Richard Burnell, canon of Haughmond

Religious priests

br. Roger Ideshale, monk of Shrewsbury
br. Roger Leton, canon of Haughmond
br. Richard Bourgh, monk of Whalley
br. Robert Parys, monk of Whalley
br. John de Dobnam, monk of Whalley
br. John del More, monk of Whalley

225.   Ordination held in Coventry cathedral by S[imon Brampton], bp.
Tripolitanensis. 19 September 1416.

Acolytes

Robert Katrik, dean of the collegiate church of St Chad, Shrewsbury
Richard Waren
John Walker
Robert Sturdy

Secular subdeacons

Robert Catrik, canon of Lichfield cathedral
John Bradwell, rector of Birdingbury
Thurstan Longley, rector of Prestwich
Thomas Salman, dioc. Lincoln, by l.d., to t. Pipewell
Roger Pottere, to t. hospital of St Giles, Shrewsbury
John Lowe, to t. hospital of St Giles, Shrewsbury
Thomas Stavndon, to t. Lilleshall
John Newman, to t. Merevale

William Sandiaker, to t. Dale
John Stevenson, to t. Wombridge
Roger Forst, to t. hospital of St John, Coventry
William Smyth, to t. Burscough
[f.37r] John Morgon, dioc. Lincoln, by l.d. to t. Gracedieu
John Roges, to t. Repton
Hugh Scolys, to t. Whalley

Secular deacons

Thomas Widenale, to t. St Mary, Sulby
John Ady, to t. Wombridge
William Bosworth, to t. Repton
John Smethurst, to t. Whalley
Robert Childe, dioc. Lincoln, by l.d., to t. Pipewell
Reginald Tarlton, to t. Burscough

Secular priests

Ralph Stanley, to t. Birkenhead
William Honte, to t. Church Gresley
Laurence Hatton, to t. Whalley
Nicholas Hyll, to t. Dale
John Gybon, to t. Tutbury
Henry Clerk, to t. Burton
John Pach, to t. Hailes
John Westley, to t. hospital of St John, Coventry
John Hatton, to t. Wombridge

Religious acolytes

br. Thomas Bristowe, O.Carm., of Coventry
br. John Stavnford, O.Carm., of Coventry

Religious subdeacons

br. Henry Hampton, O.Carm., of Coventry
br. William Rissheton, canon of Haughmond
br. Alexander Aldelem, canon of Trentham
br. Thomas Sutton, O.P., of Warwick
br. Thomas London
br. Thomas Pollesworth, monk of Coventry
br. John Northampton, monk of Coventry

Religious deacons

br. John Southam, canon of Kenilworth
br. Robert Stanton, O.Carm., of Coventry
br. John Grene, canon of Maxstoke
br. William Coudray, monk of Stoneleigh
br. John White, monk of Stoneleigh
br. Thomas Rugeley, canon of Arbury

Religious priests

[col. b] br. John Nuson, O. Carm., of Coventry
br. Richard Napton, canon of Kenilworth
br. John Burton, canon of Church Gresley

226.   Ordination held in Lichfield cathedral by Robert [Mulfield], bp. of
Killalo. 19 December 1416.

Acolytes

William Hore   John Robyns
John Clifton   John Haer
John Broun   John Assheton

Secular subdeacons

Henry Broun, to t. Burscough
Robert Normanton, to t. St Robert at Knaresborough
Giles Asteley, to t. hospital of St John, Coventry
Nicholas Wolfall, to t. Burscough
Thomas Staundon, to t. Lilleshall
Roger Clerc, to t. Baswich
John Offeley, to t. Lilleshall
Richard Waryn, to t. hospital of St John, Coventry
Robert Rose, to t. Launde[3]
John Walker, to t. Wenlock
Thomas Shukbourgh, to t. hospital of St John, Lichfield

Secular deacons

John Newman, to t. Merevale
John Bradwell, rector of Birdingbury, by l.d.
William Sandiaker, to t. Dale
John Morgon, dioc. Lincoln, by l.d., to t. Gracedieu
Roger Potter, to t. hospital of St Giles, Shrewsbury
Thomas Lowe, to t. hospital of St Giles, Shrewsbury
Thomas Salman, dioc. Lincoln, by l.d. to t. Pipewell
Roger Forst, to t. hospital of St John, Coventry
Hugh Scolys, to t. Whalley
William Smyth, to t. Burscough
John Stevenson, to t. Wombridge

Secular priests

William Bosworth, to t. Repton
[f. 37v] John Ady, to t. Wombridge
Reginald Tarlton, to t. Burscough

[3] From dioc. Lincoln, ordained without l.d.: see *The register of Bishop
Repingdon, 1405–19*, ed. M. Archer, iii (Lincoln Record Society, 74, 1982),
no. 367.

John Smethyrst, to t. Whalley
Robert Childe, dioc. Lincoln, by l.d., to t. Pipewell
Thomas Widenale, to t. St Mary, Sulby

Religious acolytes

br. William Bowell
br. Edward Bradkirke, O.F.M.
br. Thomas Neston, O.F.M.
br. John Horald, O.F.M.

Religious subdeacons

br. Walter Burgeys, O.F.M.
br. William Heyne, O.P.
br. Robert Spyne, O.Carm.
br. William Lanford, O.Carm.
br. Roger Hewster, monk of Combermere
br. Walter Hunt
br. John Duffeld, canon of Dale
br. Henry Sutton, canon of Dale

Religious deacons

br. Louis Newton, O.F.M., from Lichfield convent
br. Antony de Colonia, O.F.M., from Lichfield convent
br. Sibertus de Colonia, O.F.M., from Lichfield convent
br. William Catysby, O.P.
br. Alexander Aldelem, canon of Trentham

Religious priest

br. Thomas Derby, canon of Dale

227.   Ordination held in Lichfield cathedral by R[obert Mulfield], bp. of Killalo. 6 March 1416/17.

Acolytes

Thomas Aleyn
John Molynton
John Robynton
Thomas Steyn
Ralph de Morley
Robert Swynley
Thomas Wade
Thomas Onne

Thomas Felelot
William Haysnap
Walter Brodey
William Parker
John Stretton
Thomas Daa

[col. b] Secular subdeacons

Richard Bele, warden of the chapel of *Salbourne*, dioc. London
Henry Merland, to t. Whalley
John Assheton, to t. Dieulacres
John Heyr, to t. Ranton

William Clyfton, to t. Stoneleigh
Thomas Pope, to t. collegiate church of St Mary, Southwell
Robert Lelye, dioc. Hereford, by l.d., to t. [blank]⁴
John Pyrton, to t. Lilleshall
John Kyngeston, to t. Darley
Thomas Forst, dioc. Lincoln, by l.d., to t. St John, Northampton
John Broun, to t. Vale Royal
James Fissher, to t. Upholland

Secular deacons

Richard Waryn, to t. hospital of St John, Coventry
John Nowell, to t. hospital of St John, Coventry
Giles Asteley, to t. hospital of St John, Coventry
Roger Clerk, to t. Baswich
Robert Normanton, to t. St Robert near Knaresborough
Nicholas Wollefall, to t. Burscough
Henry Broun, to t. Burscough
Robert Rose, to t. Launde⁵
John Offeley, to t. Lilleshall

Secular priests

John Bradwell, rector of Birdingbury
Hugh Scolys, to t. Whalley
John Newman, to t. Merevale
William Smyth, to t. Burscough
Thomas Salman, dioc. Lincoln, by l.d., to t. Pipewell
Roger Forst, to t. hospital of St John, Coventry
Roger Potter, to t. hospital of St Giles, Shrewsbury
John Lowe, to t. hospital of St Giles, Shrewsbury
John Stevenson, to t. Wombridge
John Morgan, dioc. Lincoln, by l.d., to t. Gracedieu
Thomas Scawndon, to t. Lilleshall

Religious acolytes

br. John Chell, monk of Hulton

Religious subdeacons

br. William Bowell, O.F.M., from Lichfield convent
br. Henry de Colonia, O.F.M., from Lichfield convent
[f.38r] br. John Blakewey, monk of Buildwas
br. John Horold

Religious deacons

br. John Duffeld, canon of Dale

⁴ If he is to be identified with Roger Lye, this should probably read St Giles,
Shrewsbury; see below, nos. 228, 229.
⁵ See above, no. 226.

44

br. Henry Sutton, canon of Dale
br. Walter Burges

Religious priests

br. Louis Neuton, O.[F.M.], of Lichfield
br. Alexander Aldelym

228.   Ordination held in Lichfield cathedral by Robert [Mulfield], bp. of Killalo. 27 March 1417.

Acolytes

Richard Parke   Richard Claybrok
Richard Lyne   John Wodelok

Secular subdeacons

Thomas Thakar, to t. Gracedieu
William Grateford, dioc. Hereford, by l.d., to t. hospital of St James,
    Bridgnorth
John Molynton, to t. Birkenhead
Thomas Felylode, to t. St James, Bridgnorth
Thomas Steyn, to t. Burton

Secular deacons

John Pirton, to t. Lilleshall
John Heyr, to t. Ranton
Roger Lye, dioc. Hereford, by l.d., to t. hospital of St Giles, Shrewsbury
William Clifton, to t. Stoneleigh
Henry Merland, to t. Whalley
John Broun, to t. Vale Royal

Secular priests

Robert Normanton, to t. St Robert, Knaresborough
Roger Clerk, to t. Baswich
Giles Asteley, to t. hospital of St John, Coventry
William Sandiaker, to t. Dale
Robert Rose, to t. Launde[6]
John Offeley, to t. Lilleshall

[col.b] Religious subdeacons

br. Thomas Hagno, canon of Lilleshall
br. John Chedle, monk of Hulton

Religious deacons

br. William Bowell, of Lichfield convent
br. Henry de Colonia, of Lichfield convent

    [6] See no. 226.

45

Religious priests

br. Richard, monk of Burton

229.   Ordination held in the prebendal church of Eccleshall by R[obert Mulfield], bp. of Killalo. 10 April 1417.

Acolytes

Thomas Croneegge   Thomas de Coton
Ralph Stokton   Thomas Gerveys

Secular subdeacons

John Netham, to t. Rewley
John Waturhull, to t. Rocester
William Wright, to t. Markby
John Wodelok, to t. Birkenhead
John Prys, dioc. Hereford, by l.d., to t. hospital of St Giles, Shrewsbury
Richard Claybroke, to t. Stone
John Wodehous, to t. Birkenhead
David de Overton, to t. Chester
Thomas de Onne, to t. Ranton
Richard Lyne, to t. Dorchester

Secular deacons

William Grateford, dioc. Hereford, by l.d., to t. hospital of St James,
   Bridgnorth
Thomas Steyn, to t. Burton
Thomas Felilode, to t. hospital of St James, Bridgnorth
Edward Rede, rector of Yoxall, t. his benefice
John Molynton, to t. Birkenhead

[f.38v] Secular priests

Roger Lye, dioc. Hereford, by l.d., to t. hospital of St Giles, Shrewsbury
John Heyr, to t. Ranton
William Clyfton, to t. Stoneleigh

230.   Ordination held in Lichfield cathedral by R[obert Mulfield], bp. of Killalo. 5 June 1417.

Acolytes

John Pole, rector of a mediety of Walton
Henry Coke   William Kyng
Thomas Howell   Hugh Wetrev
Richard Folk   James Brid
William Legburghn

46

Secular subdeacons

William Parker, to t. Lilleshall
Thomas Fraunces, to t. Wombridge
William Legburn, canon of the collegiate church of Llanddewi-Brefi, and rector
    of *Betons Ithell*, dioc. St Davids
Thomas Smyth, to t. hospital of St John, Coventry
Thomas Aleyn, warden of the free chapel of Cresswell, dioc. Lichfield
Richard Parker, to t. Repton
John Blowdon, to t. Church Gresley
Thomas Wade, to t. Breadsall Park
Thomas Hadenall, to t. Lilleshall

Secular deacons

Richard Lyne, to t. Dorchester
John Assheton, to t. Dieulacres
John Wodehouse, to t. Birkenhead
John Wodeloke, to t. Birkenhead
James Fyssher, to t. Upholland
Thomas Thakar, to t. Gracedieu
Thomas Forst, dioc. Lincoln, by l.d., to t. hospital of St John the Baptist,
    Northampton
[col. b] John Kyngeston, to t. Darley
Richard Claybroke, to t. Stone
Roger Bower, to t. Dale
John Waterfall, to t. Rocester
John Pris, dioc. Hereford, by l.d., to t. hospital of St Giles, Shrewsbury
David Overton, to t. St Werburga, Chester
William Wryght, to t. Markby

Secular priests

Henry Broun, to t. Burscough
Thomas Steyn, to t. Burton on Trent
John Molyngton, to t. Birkenhead
John Perton, to t. Lilleshall
Edward Rede, rector of Yoxall, t. his benefice
Thomas Felylode, to t. hospital of St James, Bridgnorth

[Religious] acolytes

br. John Desford, O.S.A., of Stafford

Religious subdeacons

br. Richard Dalton, O.S.A., of Stafford
br. William Acton, monk of Combermere
br. William Lichefeld, canon of Wombridge
br. Richard Colman, canon of Baswich

Religious deacons[7]

br. Richard Hampton, O.Carm., of Coventry
br. Robert Spyney, O.Carm., of Coventry
br. William Langford, O.Carm., of Coventry
br. Roger Hewster, monk of Combermere
br. Ralph Clyderowe, monk of Whalley
br. Thomas Harden, monk of Whalley
br. Roger Nonnewyk, monk of Whalley

Religious priests

br. John Walsale, O.F.M., of Lichfield
br. John Chell, monk of Hulton

231.   [ff.38v–39r] Ordination held in Lichfield cathedral by Robert [Mulfield], bp. of Killalo. 18 September 1417.

[f.39r] Acolytes

Richard Spicer
John Wyndesovere
Henry Marchall
John Adynse
Thomas Stevynson
Robert Sonky

William Bryne
Richard Sutte
Gilbert Blevyn
Thomas Cowley
John Walker
Richard Wych

Secular subdeacons

Robert Sturdy, rector of Southam, t. his benefice
James Bridde, to t. Whalley
John Lawe, to t. Burscough
Richard Mos, to t. hospital of St John, Lichfield
Robert Swynley, to t. Birkenhead
Hugh Wetreve, to t. Croxden
John Pole, rector of a mediety of Walton, dioc. Lincoln, by l.d., t. his benefice
Richard Brabson, dioc. Lincoln, by l.d., to t. Sulby
John Robyns, to t. hospital of St John, Coventry
William Hachet, dioc. Lincoln, by l.d., to t. hospital of St John, Coventry
Thomas Howell, to t. hospital of St James, Bridgnorth
Thomas Brabson, dioc. Lincoln, by l.d., to t. Sulby

Secular deacons

Thomas Smyth, to t. hospital of St John, Coventry
William Parker, to t. Lilleshall
Thomas Frances, to t. Wombridge
Thomas Pope, to t. collegiate church of St Mary, Southwell
Thomas Hodenall, to t. Lilleshall
John Blowdon, to t. Church Gresley
Thomas Onne, to t. Ranton

[7] Originally described in the heading as seculars, but that is crossed out.

48

Richard Parker, to t. Repton
Thomas Wade, to t. Breadsall Park

[col. b] Secular priests

John Waterfall, to t. Rocester
John Assheton, to t. Dieulacres
Thomas Thakar, to t. Gracedieu
John Kyngeston, to t. Darley
John Nowell, to t. hospital of St John, Coventry
William Wright, to t. Markby
James Fissher, to t. Upholland
Thomas Forst, dioc. Lincoln, by l.d., to t. hospital of St John, Northampton
Richard Claybroke, to t. Stone
John Prys, dioc. Hereford, by l.d., to t. hospital of St Giles, Shrewsbury
John Wodeloke, to t. Birkenhead
John Wodehouse, to t. Birkenhead
Richard Waryn, to t. hospital of St John, Coventry

Religious subdeacons

br. Thomas Bourgh, monk of Combe
br. John Boleton, canon of Darley
br. Thomas Bradesale, canon of Darley
br. Thomas Grene, canon of Darley
br. Henry Vernon, of Atherstone
br. Thomas Rotteley, monk of Stoneleigh

Religious deacons

br. Richard Dalton, of Warrington
br. David Lowe, canon of Norton[8]
br. Richard Bulkeley, canon of Norton
br. Henry de Lee, canon of Norton[8]
br. Henry Torefote, canon of Norton[8]
br. William Coton, canon of Norton[8]
br. Richard Burnell, canon of Haughmond[9]
br. Hugh de Leton, canon of Haughmond[8]
br. William Lichefeld, canon of Wombridge
br. John Ayleward, of Atherstone
br. John White, monk of Stoneleigh[9]

Religious priests

br. Henry Denton, O.F.M., of Lichfield
br. John Grene, canon of Maxstoke
br. John Coventre, monk of Combe
br. Thomas Lodlowe, monk of Shrewsbury
[br.] Ralph Clyderowe, monk of Whalley
br. Roger Nennewik, monk of Whalley

[8] Properly subdeacons: all appear later being ordained deacon (see index).
[9] Properly priests: see index.

49

232.   [f. 39v] Ordination held in Lichfield cathedral by Robert [Mulfield], bp. of Killalo. 18 December 1417.

Acolytes

William Bolde	Richard Wynslowe
Geoffrey Feidyn	John Temside
Thomas Cholmeley	William Merser
John Robyns	Hugh Mankok
Giles Hide	Richard de Lee
John Lane	Hugh Spencer
Adam Smyth	Geoffrey Milward
John Danby	
Thomas Drayton	

Secular subdeacons

Robert Sonke, to t. Birkenhead
William Bruyne, to t. St Werburga, Chester
William Haysnap, to t. Burscough
Thomas Stevenson, to t. Ranton
Robert Lyne, to t. Bordesley
Richard Spycer, to t. St John, Lichfield
Thomas Cowley, to t. Ranton
Ralph Morley, to t. Repton
William Porter, dioc. Lincoln, by l.d., to t. hospital of St John, Leicester
Ed. Warde, to t. Felley
William Bertton, to t. hospital of St Giles,[10] Shrewsbury
Henry Coke, to t. Upholland

Secular deacons

John Lawe, to t. Burscough
Richard Mos, to t. hospital of St John the Baptist, Lichfield
William Hachet, dioc. Lincoln, by l.d., to t. hospital of St John, Coventry
James Bridde, to t. Whalley
Thomas Brabson, dioc. Lincoln, by l.d., to t. Sulby
Hugh Wetreve, to t. Croxden
Thomas Howell, to t. hospital of St J[ames], Bridgnorth
Richard Brabson, dioc. Lincoln, by l.d., to t. Sulby
Thomas Aleyn, rector of Cresswell, dioc. Coventry and Lichfield, t. his benefice
[col. b] John Robyns, to t. hospital of St John, Coventry
John Walker, to t. Wenlock
Robert Swynley, to t. Birkenhead
William Legburn, canon of Llanddewi-Brefi collegiate church and rector of
    Betons Ithell, t. his benefices

Secular priests

Thomas Frances, to t. Wombridge

---

[10] MS: James.

50

Thomas Smyth, to t. hospital of St John, Coventry
Richard Parker, to t. Repton
John Blowdon, to t. Church Gresley
Thomas Onne, to t. Ranton
William Parker, to t. Lilleshall
Thomas Wade, to t. Breadsall Park
Richard Lyne, to t. Dorchester

Religious subdeacons

br. John Dysford, of Stafford
br. John Wenlock, of Lichfield convent
br. Robert Brompton, canon of Rocester
br. William Smyth, canon of Rocester
br. John Harley, canon of Repton
br. John Neuton, canon of Repton
br. John Repyndon, canon of Repton

Religious priests

br. Henry Hampton, O.Carm.
br. Richard Longford, O.Carm.
br. Richard Dalton
br. John Moreton

233.   Ordination held in Lichfield cathedral by R[obert Mulfield], bp. of Killalo. 19 February 1417/18.

Acolytes

Richard Malka	John Tailour
Laurence Braybon	Thomas Savage
Nicholas Ipstones	Robert Baker
Richard Wolaston	John Spencer
William Davers	John Elyot
John Savage	John Elyot

[f.40r] Secular subdeacons

Thomas Cholmeley, to t. Combermere
John Temsede, dioc. St Davids, by l.d., to t. hospital of St John, Ludlow
Richard Lee, to t. St Werburga, Chester
John Walker, dioc. Hereford, by l.d., to t. hospital of St Giles, Shrewsbury
Thomas Drayton, to t. Wombridge
Hugh Spencer, dioc. Lincoln, by l.d., to t. Launde
Robert Fissher, to t. Launde[11]
Richard Wynslowe, dioc. Lincoln, by l.d., to t. St Mary de Pratis, Leicester

[11] MS: *Landa*, but probably Upholland; see nos. 234, 235.

51

Secular deacons

William Briton, to t. hospital of St Giles,[12] Shrewsbury
Richard Spicer, to t. hospital of St John, Lichfield
William Witherley, rector of Thorp Constantine, t. his benefice
Robert Lyne, to t. Bordesley
Thomas Stevenson, to t. Ranton
Thomas Cowley, to t. Ranton
John Tailour, dioc. Lincoln, by l.d., to t. Gracedieu
William Haysnap, to t. Burscough
Ralph Morley, to t. Repton
Henry Coke, to t. Upholland
William Bruyne, to t. St Werburga, Chester
William Porter, dioc. Lincoln, by l.d., to t. hospital of St John, Leicester

Secular priests

Thomas Hadenall, to t. Lilleshall
Thomas Walker, to t. Wenlock
Richard Mos, to t. hospital of St John, Lichfield
John Lawe, to t. Burscough
James Bridde, to t. Whalley
Thomas Brabson, dioc. Lincoln, by l.d., to t. Sulby
Hugh Wetreve, to t. Croxden
Thomas Howell, to t. hospital of St James, Bridgnorth
John Robyns, to t. hospital of St John, Coventry
Thomas [Aleyn], rector of Cresswell chapel
[col. b] Richard Braybon, dioc. Lincoln, by l.d., to t. Sulby
Robert Swynley, to t. Birkenhead

Religious subdeacons

br. Thomas Holand, canon of Breadsall Park
br. John Bromeley, canon of Rocester
br. John Barowe, O.S.A., of Atherstone

Religious deacons

br. David Lowe, canon of Norton
br. Henry Torfote, canon of Norton
br. William Coton, canon of Norton
br. John Harley, canon of Repton
br. John Neuton, canon of Repton
br. John de Repdon, canon of Repton
br. Hugh Leton, canon of Haughmond
br. William Smyth, canon of Rocester
br. Robert Bromton, canon of Rocester
br. Henry Vernon, O.S.A., of Atherstone
br. John Dysford, O.S.A., of Stafford[13]

[12] MS: James.

[13] MS: Atherstone, but see nos. 232, 234.

Religious priests

br. William Lichefeld, canon of Wombridge
br. John Aylleward, O.S.A., of Atherstone
br. Thomas More, monk of Burton
br. Nicholas Warde, monk of Burton
br. Thomas Norton, monk of Burton
br. Henry Asshebourne, monk of Burton

234. Ordination held in Lichfield cathedral by R[obert Mulfield], bp. of Killalo. 12 March 1417/18.

Acolytes

Thomas Baker	William Verney
John Prest	Robert Barton

Secular subdeacons

Richard Wolaston, to t. Birkenhead
John Elyot, to t. Repton
Laurence Braybon, to t. Tutbury
[f.40v] Robert Barton, dioc. Lincoln, by l.d., to t. Gracedieu
John Tailour, to t. Breadsall Park
Richard Malcane, to t. Worksop

Secular deacons

Thomas Cholmeley, to t. Combermere
Gilbert Blene, to t. Birkenhead
John Hurst, to t. Hailes
Hugh Spencer, dioc. Lincoln, by l.d., to t. Launde
Robert Fissher, to t. Upholland
John Walker, dioc. Hereford, by l.d., to t. hospital of St Giles, Shrewsbury
John Temsete, dioc. St Davids, by l.d., to t. hospital of St John, Ludlow
Richard Longnore, dioc. Hereford, by l.d., to t. St Giles, Shrewsbury
John Wyndesovere, to t. Rocester
John Grenehode, to t. Birkenhead

Secular priests

William Witherley, rector of Thorp Constantine
Richard Spicer, to t. hospital of St John, Lichfield
Robert Lyne, to t. Bordesley
John Tailour, dioc. Lincoln, by l.d., to t. Gracedieu
William Beriton, to t. hospital of St Giles, Shrewsbury
William Haysnape, to t. Burscough
Henry [Coke], to t. Upholland
Robert Sonky, to t. Birkenhead
William Bruyne, to t. St Werburga, Chester
Thomas Cowley, to t. Ranton
Thomas Stevenson, to t. Ranton

Religious subdeacons

br. John Rasyn, O.S.A., of Stafford
br. Roger Fox, canon of Beauchief
br. John Fereby, canon of Beauchief

Religious deacons

br. Thomas Holand, canon of Breadsall Park

Religious priests

br. John Dysford, O.S.A., of Stafford
br. Robert Bromton, canon of Rocester

235.   [col. b] Ordination held in Lichfield cathedral by R[obert Mulfield], bp. of Killalo. 26 March 1418.

Secular subdeacons

John Adyns, to t. Ranton

Secular deacons

Richard Wolaston, to t. Birkenhead
Robert Sturdy, rector of Southam, t. his benefice
Robert Barton, dioc. Lincoln, by l.d., to t. Gracedieu
Richard Malcane, to t. Worksop
Thomas Drayton, to t. Wombridge
Thomas Cay, to t. St Giles, Shrewsbury

Secular priests

John Walker, dioc. Hereford, by l.d., to t. hospital of St Giles, Shrewsbury
Thomas Cholmeley, to t. Combermere
John Temsete, dioc. St Davids, by l.d., to t. hospital of St John, Ludlow
Robert Fissher, to t. Upholland
John Hurst, to t. Hailes

Religious priests

br. John, O.F.M., of Nottingham

236.   Ordination held in Lichfield cathedral by R[obert Mulfield], bp. of Killalo. 21 May 1418.

Acolytes

John[14] Verney   John Hechekyn
John Walkeden   Richard Herby
John Dawkyn   Roger Averay

[14] Properly Philip? See nos. 237, 239, 240.

William Kemsay
William Peche
John Belamy
William Ruyton
William Claxton

Roger Draycote
William Saxby
Henry Bolton

[f.41r] Secular subdeacons

John de Radeclif, to t. Whalley
Henry Shirwalacres, to t. Burscough
John Roby, to t. Birkenhead
John Broun, to t. Rocester
Thomas Coton, to t. St Werburga, Chester
John Elyot, to t. Dale
John Spencer, to t. Repton
Robert Rendant, to t. *Wodenassh*
John Normanton, to t. Felley

Secular deacons

John Pole, rector of a mediety of Walton, dioc. Lincoln, by l.d., t. his benefice
John Tailour, to t. Breadsall Park
John Fleccher, to t. Whalley
John Elyot, to t. Repton
Matthew Kelcheth, to t. Burscough
Ed. Warde, to t. Felley
Thurstan Longley, rector of Prestwich, dioc. Lichfield, t. his benefice
Laurence Braybon, to t. Tutbury
John Adyns, to t. Ranton
Richard Wynslowe, dioc. Lincoln, by l.d., to t. St Mary de Pratis, Leicester

Secular priests

Hugh Spencer, dioc. Lincoln, by l.d., to t. Launde
Richard Wolaston, to t. Birkenhead
Nicholas Wollefall, to t. Burscough
Gilbert Blene, to t. Birkenhead
Richard Langnore, dioc. Hereford, by l.d., to t. St Giles, Shrewsbury
Robert Barton, dioc. Lincoln, by l.d., to t. Gracedieu
Thomas Drayton, to t. Wombridge
Thomas Cay, to t. St Giles, Shrewsbury
Robert Sturdy, rector of Southam, t. his benefice
Richard Grenehode, to t. Birkenhead
William Porter, dioc. Lincoln, by l.d., to t. hospital of St John, Leicester
John Wyndesovere, to t. Rocester

Religious acolytes

br. John White, canon of Maxstoke
br. Laurence Perepoynt, monk of Upholland

Religious subdeacons

br. John Cressewell, of Warrington convent
br. John Wode, monk of Shrewsbury
br. William Beston, canon of Lilleshall
br. Richard Braynoke, monk of St Anne near Coventry
br. Nicholas Burscogh, monk of Upholland

Religious deacons

br. Thomas Hagno, canon of Lilleshall
br. John Blakeway, monk of Buildwas
br. John Southam, canon of Kenilworth
br. William Caudray, monk of Stoneleigh
br. Richard Colman, canon of Baswich
br. John Bulton, canon of Darley
br. Thomas Bradeshall, canon of Darley
br. Thomas Grene, canon of Darley
br. Thomas Bourgh, monk of Combe

Religious priests

br. Thomas London, monk of Coventry cathedral
br. John Aston, monk of Shrewsbury
br. Thomas Holand, canon of Breadsall Park

237.   Ordination held in Lichfield cathedral by R[obert Mulfield], bp. of Killalo. 24 September 1418.

Acolytes

William Inse, rector of Sparham, dioc. Norwich
Adam Broun   John Asteley
William Bele   Robert Lanselyn
Robert Gedlyng   John Wotley
                                Richard Prymmerose

Secular subdeacons

William Inse, rector of Sparham, dioc. Norwich, t. his benefice
Ranulf Mason, vicar in the collegiate church of St John, Chester
Henry de Bolton, to t. Whalley
Adam de Fere, to t. Whalley
John Belamy, to t. Vale Royal
Thomas Savage, rector of Checkley, t. his benefice
[f.41v] John Hochyn, to t. St Mary de Pratis, Leicester
Richard Mos, to t. Burscough
Henry Toppyng, to t. Burscough
Thomas Raynforth, to t. Upholland
Thomas Dichefeld, to t. Upholland
Thomas Bolton, dioc. York, by l.d., to t. Selby
William Ive, to t. hospital of St John, Coventry

John Fissher, dioc. York, by l.d., to t. Combe
Thomas Coton, to t. St Werburga, Chester
John Welinton, to t. Whalley
Philip Verney, to t. Rocester
William Kemsay, to t. Ranton
John Coventre, to t. Whalley
John Trewman, rector of Patching, dioc. Canterbury, t. his benefice

Secular deacons

John Broun, to t. Rocester
M. John Coton, LL.B., dioc. York, by l.d., to t. Cockersand
John Normanton, to t. Felley
Robert Hill, dioc. Worcester, by l.d., to t. St Radegunde, Thelsford
John Roby, to t. Birkenhead
John Radeclif, to t. Whalley
Henry Shirwalacres, to t. Burscough
John Elyot, to t. Repton[15]
Henry Boydell, rector of Standon, dioc. Coventry, t. his benefice
John Spencer, to t. Repton
Thurstan Longley, rector of Prestwich, dioc. Lichfield, t. his benefice

Secular priests

Richard Malcane, to t. Worksop
Roger Bowher, to t. Dale
John Fleccher, to t. Whalley
Laurence Braybon, to t. Tutbury
Ed. Warde, to t. Felley
[col. b] John Elyot, to t. Repton
John Pole, rector of a mediety of Walton, dioc. Lincoln, by l.d., t. his benefice
John Tailour, to t. Breadsall Park
Richard Wynslowe, dioc. Lincoln, by l.d., to t. St Mary de Pratis, Leicester
William Hachet, dioc. Lincoln, by l.d., to t. hospital of St John, Coventry
John Adyns, to t. Ranton

Religious subdeacons

br. Laurence Forbrig, O.S.A., of Stafford
br. John Trevers, O.F.M., of Lichfield
br. John Godefelowe, monk of Dieulacres
br. John Henschawe, monk of Dieulacres
br. John White, canon of Maxstoke

Religious deacons

br. John Cressale, O.S.A., of Warrington
br. Roger Fox, canon of Beauchief
br. John Selby, canon of Beauchief
br. Ed. Brendurgas, O.F.M., of Lichfield

[15] Properly Dale, see nos. 236, 238.

br. John Wode, monk of St Peter's, Shrewsbury
br. Richard Braynoke, monk of St Anne near Coventry
br. John Bromley, canon of Rocester
br. Richard Glouceter, canon of Arbury
br. Richard Shiplode, canon of Arbury
br. Thomas Stonley, monk of Stoneleigh

Religious priests

br. John Bredon, canon of Church Gresley
br. Robert Melbourne, canon of Church Gresley

238.   Ordination held in Lichfield cathedral by Robert [Mulfield], bp. of Killalo. 17 December 1418.

[f.42r] Acolytes,

Reginald Neuton
William Horley
William Gerard
William Fissher
John Gerard

Richard Cosyn
John Coke
Richard Tolle
Thomas Lancastreshire
John Smyth

Secular subdeacons

Robert Lancelyn, to t. Burscough
Robert Blondell, to t. Burscough
John Robyns, to t. Bridgnorth
Robert Baker, to t. nuns of Polesworth
John Bosedon, to t. Dieulacres
John Kyng, dioc. Lincoln, by l.d., to t. Owston
John Savage, to t. Vale Royal
John Oteley, to t. Haughmond
Richard Prymmerose, to t. Vale Royal
Nicholas Wall, to t. Burscough

Secular deacons

Adam de Fere, to t. Whalley
Henry Bolton, to t. Whalley
William Kemsay, to t. Ranton
John de Coventre, to t. Whalley
Thomas Bolton, dioc. York, by l.d., to t. Selby
John Elleswike, rector of Castle Rising, dioc. Norwich, t. his benefice
Thomas Raynforth, to t. Upholland
Thomas Dichefeld, to t. Upholland
John Belamy, to t. Vale Royal
Henry Toppyng, to t. Burscough
Richard Lee, to t. St Werburga, Chester
John Fissher, dioc. York, by l.d., to t. Combe
John Hochyn, to t. St Mary de Pratis, Leicester

Richard Mos, to t. Burscough

Secular priests

M. John Coton, LL.B., dioc. York, by l.d., to t. Cockersand
John de Radeclif, to t. Whalley
John Roby, to t. Birkenhead
Henry Shirwalacres, to t. Burscough
Robert Hyll, dioc. Worcester, by l.d., to t. St Radegunde, Thelsford
[col. b] John Elyot, to t. Dale
John Normanton, to t. Felley
Ralph Morley, to t. Repton
John Spencer, to t. Repton
Thomas Coton, to t. St Werburga, Chester

Religious acolytes

br. William Langford, O.P., of Newcastle
br. Thomas Clifton, canon of Church Gresley

Religious subdeacons

br. Edward Bradkirke, O.F.M., of Lichfield
br. Ralph Pepepoynt, monk of Upholland

Religious deacons

br. John Rasyn, of Stafford convent
br. Laurence Forbrig, of Stafford convent
br. Henry Lee, canon of Norton
br. Thomas Bromwich, O.F.M., of Lichfield
br. Nicholas Burscogh, monk of Upholland

Religious priests

br. John Cressall, of Warrington
br. David Lowe, canon of Norton
br. Henry Torfote, canon of Norton
br. William Coton, canon of Norton
br. William Rissheton, canon of Haughmond
br. Thomas Rugeley, canon of Arbury
br. Richard Gloucestre, canon of Arbury
br. Richard Breynok, monk of St Anne near Coventry

239.   Ordination held in Lichfield cathedral by Robert [Mulfield], bp. of Killalo. 11 March 1418/19.

Acolytes

Edward Claydon   John Sotheworth
Richard Herby   Thomas Batman
Henry Knyghton   Thomas Hendon
[f.42v] John Snell   Roger Wode

Thomas Prossell   Roger Carter
Richard Velleworth   William Beche

  Secular subdeacons

Thomas Cronage, to t. Ranton
Hugh Mankoc, to t. Trentham
Richard Cosyn, to t. Burscough
John Bikkenhill, to t. Clattercote
M. William Bolde, LL.B., to t. patrimony
William Massam, dioc. York, by l.d., to t. Jervaulx
Laurence Faryngton, to t. hospital of St John, Lichfield
William Meghhen, to t. hospital of St Giles, Shrewsbury
Thomas Bonell, to t. Birkenhead
John Ronynton, to t. King's Mead
John Love, to t. Repton
William Idell, to t. hospital of St John Baptist, Northampton, for all orders
John Gerard, to t. hospital of St John, Coventry
William Harley, to t. hospital of St John, Lichfield
Thomas Betteley, to t. Arbury
Richard Tailour, to t. Whalley
Thomas Erkale, to t. hospital of St James, Bridgnorth

  Secular deacons

John Belington, to t. Whalley
John Robyns, to t. St James, Bridgnorth
John Bosedon, to t. Dieulacres
William Ive, to t. hospital of St John Baptist, Coventry
John Kyng, dioc. Lincoln, by l.d., to t. Owston
Philip Verney, to t. Rocester
John Oteley, to t. Haughmond
Richard Prymrose, to t. Vale Royal
Nicholas Wall, to t. Burscough
Robert Blundell, to t. Burscough

  Secular priests

Thomas Bolton, dioc. York, by l.d., to t. Selby
John Belamy, to t. Vale Royal
John Broun, to t. Rocester
Thomas Dichefeld, to t. Upholland
Henry Toppyng, to t. Burscough
[col. b] Thomas Raynford, to t. Upholland
Henry Boidell, rector of Standon, t. his benefice
John Hochyn, to t. St Mary de Pratis, Leicester
Richard Mosse, to t. Burscough
John Fissher, to t. Combe
Henry Bolton, to t. Whalley
John de Coventre, to t. Whalley
William Kemsay, to t. Ranton

Adam de Fere, to t. Whalley

Religious acolytes

br. John Lye
br. John Cleydon
br. Philip Stafford

Religious subdeacons

br. William Langford, O.P., of Newcastle
br. Stephen Sharp, monk of Combe
br. Thomas Clifton, canon of Church Gresley

Religious deacons

br. John Suderman, O.F.M., of Northampton
br. Geoffrey Herford, O.P., of Northampton
br. Howell Forest, O.P., of Shrewsbury
br. John White, canon of Maxstoke
[br.] Carmelius Jacobi, O.F.M., of Nottingham

Religious priests

br. William Rothewell, O.F.M., of Northampton
br. Richard Langford, O.F.M., of Northampton
br. John Rasyn, O.P., of Stafford
br. Laurence Forberg, O.P., of Stafford
br. Thomas Bromwich, O.F.M., of Lichfield
br. Thomas Burgh, monk of Combe
br. John Hanbury, canon of Rocester
br. John Blakewey

240.   Ordination held in Lichfield cathedral by Robert [Mulfield], bp. of
Killalo. 1 April 1419.

[f.43r] Acolytes

William Bokelond   William Preston
Thomas Barbot   Thomas Walker
Henry Clayton   Thomas Lowe

Secular subdeacons

Thomas Piers, dioc. Lincoln, by l.d., to t. Gracedieu
Thomas Lancastreshire, to t. hospital of St John Baptist, Warwick
John Sotheworth, to t. St Werburga, Chester
Geoffrey Milner, to t. Lilleshall
Henry Clayton, dioc. Coventry and Lichfield, rector of Northmoor, dioc.
    Lincoln, t. his benefice

Secular deacons

John Gerard, to t. hospital of St John, Coventry
Hugh Mankoc, to t. Trentham
Richard Cosyn, to t. Burscough

Thomas Cronage, to t. Ranton
M. William Bolde, LL.B., by l.d., t. his father's patrimony
William Massam, dioc. York, by l.d., to t. Jervaulx
Thomas Bonell, to t. Birkenhead
John Love, to t. Repton
William Meghhen, to t. hospital of St Giles, Shrewsbury
Richard Tailour, to t. Whalley
Thomas Erkale, to t. hospital of St James, Bridgnorth

Secular priests

John Robyns, to t. St James, Bridgnorth
Philip Verney, to t. Rocester
Robert Blundell, to t. Burscough
John Kyng, dioc. Lincoln, by l.d., to t. Owston
Robert Lancelyn, to t. Burscough

Religious subdeacons

br. Philip Stafford, canon of Stone
br. William Mustelwike, [O.E.S.A.],[16] of Atherstone
br. John Peynter, [O.E.S.A.],[16] of Atherstone

Religious deacons

br. John Borgh, [O.E.S.A.],[16] of Atherstone
br. Thomas Clifton, canon of Church Gresley

Religious priests

br. Geoffrey Herford, O.P., of Northampton
br. Henry Vernon, [O.E.S.A.],[16] of Atherstone

241. [col. b] Ordination held in Lichfield cathedral by Robert [Mulfield], bp. of Killalo. 15 April 1419.

Acolytes

Richard Belle   William Heyne
John Forton   William Cardemaker

Secular subdeacons

William de Prestbury, to t. Dieulacres
John Snell, to t. Whalley
William Heyne, to t. Stoneleigh

Secular deacons

John Sotheworth, to t. St Werburga, Chester
John Ronyngton, to t. Kings Mead
Thomas Lancastreshir, to t. hospital of St John Baptist, Warwick

[16] The MS gives the order as O.P., but there was no Dominican house at Atherstone.

Secular priests

William Massam, dioc. York, by l.d., to t. Jervaulx
Thomas Erkalle, to t. St James, Bridgnorth
Thomas Cronage, to t. Ranton
Thomas Bonell, to t. Birkenhead
John Oteley, to t. Haughmond
M. William Bolde, to t. his father's patrimony

Religious deacons

br. William Longford, O.P., of Newcastle
br. William Mustulwike, [O.E.S.A.],[17] of Atherstone

Religious priests

br. Thomas Clifton, canon of Church Gresley

242. Ordination held in Lichfield cathedral by Robert [Mulfield], bp. of Killalo. 11 June 1419.

[f.43v] Acolytes

Robert Curteys	John Snowe
Walter Broun	Robert Elmeton
Richard Hert	John Chedwike
Laurence Bate	

Secular subdeacons

Richard Bosvyll, to t. Nuneaton
Richard Herve, to t. Vale Royal
Hugh Parker, to t. Whalley
Richard Dugdale, to t. Sawley
Robert Tolle, to t. Hailes
Richard Bee, to t. Roger de Bradschawe, esq., lord of Meynell Langley
John Longdon, to t. hospital of St Giles, Shrewsbury
Thomas Stanyhurst, to t. Burscough
Ralph Schagh, to t. Catesby
William Clayton, to t. Crowland
William Hore, to t. Catesby
William Cardemaker, to t. hospital of St James, Bridgnorth, for all orders
Richard Falke, to t. Wombridge
William Loweles, to t. Burscough

Secular deacons

Thomas Piers, dioc. Lincoln, by l.d., to t. Gracedieu
Geoffrey Milner, to t. Lilleshall
William Presbury, to t. Dieulacres
Laurence Faryngton, to t. hospital of St John, Lichfield

---

[17] See note 16.

John Bikenhill, to t. Clattercote
Henry Clayton, rector of Northmoor, dioc. Lincoln, t. his benefice
William Harley, to t. hospital of St John, Lichfield
William Idell, dioc. Lincoln, by l.d., to t. St John Baptist, Northampton
John Snell, to t. Whalley
William Heyne, to t. Stoneleigh

Secular priests
[col. b] Matthew Kelcheth, to t. Burscough
John Bosedon, to t. Dieulacres
Hugh Monkoc, to t. Trentham
Richard Lee, to t. St Werburga, Chester
John Gerard, to t. hospital of St John, Coventry
Richard Cosyn, to t. Burscough
William Ive, to t. hospital of St John, Coventry
John Love, to t. Repton
William Meghen, to t. hospital of St Giles, Shrewsbury
Richard Prymrose, to t. Vale Royal
John Sotheworth, to t. St Werburga, Chester
John Belington, to t. Whalley
John Ronyngton, to t. Kings Mead
Nicholas Wall, to t. Burscough
John Elswike, rector of Castle Rising
Richard Tailour, to t. Whalley
Thomas Lancastershire, to t. hospital of St John Baptist, Warwick

Religious acolytes

br. Richard Barnvil
br. Thomas Huntar, O.P., of Warwick
br. Robert Burton, O.P., of Warwick
br. William Grant, O.P., of Warwick

Religious subdeacons

br. Thomas Prync, canon of Lilleshall
br. Samson Goldyng, monk of Birkenhead
br. Richard Neston[18]
br. Nicholas Chatburn[18]

Religious deacons

br. Philip Stafford, canon of Stone
br. William Beyston, canon of Lilleshall
br. John Peyntour, [O.E.S.A.],[19] of Atherstone

---

[18] Later additions. It is not clear whether they were also monks of Birkenhead, or whether the bracket against their name applies to them alone, in which case they may have been friars.
[19] MS describes them as O.P., but there was no Dominican house at Atherstone.

[Religious] priests

br. Thomas Hagno, canon of Lilleshall
br. Thomas Harden, monk of Whalley
br. John[20] Mustelwike, [O.E.S.A.],[21] of Atherstone
br. John Borowe, [O.E.S.A.],[21] of Atherstone
br. John Southam, canon of Kenilworth
br. John Wode, monk of Shrewsbury
br. Matthew Yonge, O.F.M., Oxford

243.   [f.44r] Ordination held in Lichfield cathedral by Robert [Mulfield], bp. of Killalo. 23 September 1419.

Acolytes

Thomas Stoke   Hugh Berdemore
Thomas Clyff   Richard Pennesby
William Ustanes   Roger Bayly

Secular subdeacons

John Crossepeny, by l.d., to t. Whalley
John Prest, to t. Polesworth
Roger Wordulworth, to t. Valle Crucis
Nicholas Ipstans, to t. Lilleshall
Thomas Tuy, to t. Owston
Richard Prise, to t. hospital of St Giles, Shrewsbury
John Chadwyk, to t. Whalley
William Gerard, to t. Stoneleigh
William Bradney, to t. Buildwas
Robert Elmeton, to t. Canwell

Secular deacons

William Inse, rector of Sparham, dioc. Norwich
Thomas Stanyhirst, to t. Burscough
William Hore, to t. Catesby
Richard Herve, to t. Vale Royal
Richard Bee, to t. Roger de Bradschawe, esq., lord of Longley
Robert Tolle, to t. Hailes
John Longdon, to t. hospital of St Giles, Shrewsbury
Hugh Parker, to t. Whalley
William Loweles, to t. Burscough
Ralph Schagh, to t. Catesby
Richard Bosvyle, to t. Nuneaton
William Cardemaker, to t. hospital of St James,[22] Bridgnorth
Richard Dugdale, to t. Sawley
Richard Falke, to t. Wombridge
William Clayton, to t. St Frideswide, Oxford

[20] Properly William: see above, nos. 240, 241.

[21] See note 19   [22] MS: Giles

Secular priests

[col. b] Thomas Piers, dioc. Lincoln, by l.d., to t. Gracedieu
John Bikkenhull, to t. Clattercote
Geoffrey Milner, to t. Lilleshall
Laurence Faryngton, to t. hospital of St John, Lichfield
William Idell, dioc. Lincoln, by l.d., to t. hospital of St John Baptist,
    Northampton
John Snell, to t. Whalley
William Harley, to t. hospital of St John, Lichfield
William Prestbury, to t. Dieulacres

Religious acolytes

br. John Marys

Religious subdeacons

br. Denis Flynt

Religious deacons

br. Laurence Perepoynt, monk of Upholland

Religious priests

br. Nicholas Burscogh, monk of Upholland
br. John Musche, O.F.M., of Lichfield
br. William Bowell, O.F.M., of Lichfield
br. Ralph Leylond, monk of Croxden
br. John Peynter, O.S.A., of Atherstone
br. Richard Lichefeld, canon of Repton
br. Philip Stafford, canon of Stone

244.   Ordination held in Lichfield cathedral by Robert [Mulfield], bp. of
Killalo. 24 December 1419.

Acolytes

Stephen de Longley	Stephen Janyn
Roger de Endon	Nicholas Lathum
Thomas Loxley	Richard Warmynton
John Harpere	Adam Whitstone

Secular subdeacons

Richard Massy, to t. Vaudey
Christopher Wyndyn, to t. Kings Mead
[f.44v] William Bukland, to t. Combermere
Thomas Hule, to t. Whalley
Nicholas Derby, to t. Charley
William Tapley, to t. Kings Mead
John Bone, to t. Vale Royal

John de Heton, to t. Whalley
Ranulf de Tildesley, to t. Burscough
Richard Smyth, to t. Stoneleigh
Thomas Loxley, to t. hospital of St John, Coventry
Thomas Lacheford, to t. Hailes
Thomas Cliffe, to t. Basingwerk
Adam Smyth, to t. Birkenhead
Henry More, to t. Hailes
Richard Hervy, to t. Darley
William Evston, to t. Buildwas
Thomas Robyns, to t. hospital of St James, Bridgnorth
John Hechecok, to t. Buildwas
Robert Staresmore, to t. Hailes

Secular deacons

Thomas Savage, rector of Checkley, dioc. Li[chfield]
Thomas Curson, rector of Pipewell, dioc. Lincoln
John Prest, to t. Polesworth
William Gerard, to t. Stoneleigh
John Crossepeny, to t. Whalley
John Savage, to t. Vale Royal
Thomas Tuy, to t. Owston
William Bradney, to t. Buildwas
Robert Elmeton, to t. Canwell
Iblo Langford, rector of Nailstone, dioc. Lincoln, by l.d., t. his benefice
John Chadwike, to t. Whalley
Nicholas Ipstones, to t. Lilleshall

Secular priests

Richard Bee, to t. Roger de Bradschawe, esq., lord of Longley
William Hore, to t. Catesby
Hugh Parker, to t. Whalley
Richard Bosevile, to t. Nuneaton
William Loweles, to t. Burscough
Richard Herve, to t. Vale Royal
Robert Tolle, to t. Hailes
Richard Dugdale, to t. Whalley[23]
William Cardemaker, to t. hospital of St James,[24] Bridgnorth
[col. b] Richard Falke, to t. Wombridge
Thomas Stanyhurst, to t. Burscough
John Longdon, to t. hospital of St Giles, Shrewsbury

Religious subdeacons

br. William Hawes
br. John Kirkham

[23] Sic, but should probably be Sawley; see nos. 242, 243
[24] MS: Giles

67

br. Thomas Clifton
br. John Deyne
br. Denis Fulham

Religious deacons

br. John Wenlok

INDEX

In dealing with personal names, all variants of surnames are indexed, with cross-references to the form under which they are gathered, unless they would be adjacent to the adopted standard. At that point, all variants are shown after the adopted standard form in ( ). For place names in England and Wales, only the modern form is indexed; but the spellings which occur in the manuscript, if different, are then gathered together in []. The county is also indicated, according to the pre-1974 boundaries. Progression through the ordination lists is shown by indicating the order received (a = acolyte, s = subdeacon, d = deacon, p = priest) before the entry number, e.g. a: 219, s: 221, d: 223, p: 224. In addition to the abbreviations used in the main text, those for the progress through orders, and self-explanatory abbreviations of county names, the following additional abbreviations are used in indicating posts held: pt. = priest, r. = rector, v. = vicar.

Abyndon, br. John, O.Carm., of
    Coventry d: 224
Acton, br. William. monk of
    Combermere s: 230
Ade (Ady), John a: 221, s: 224, d: 225,
    p: 226
admission to benefices see institutions to
    benefices
admission to prebend xi, 218
Admondeston, Thomas. r. Forton;
    prebendal v. of Prees 109
Admondeston, M. William. master of
    Tong college 138
Ady see Ade
Adyns (Adynse), John a: 231, s: 235, d:
    236, p: 237
affinity see dispensations
Albano, Italy, bp. of see Orsini, Jordan
Albrighton, Salop, vicarage 149
    vicar of see Wodehouse, Richard
Aldelem (Aldelym), br. Alexander. canon
    of Trentham a: 224, s: 225, d: 226,
    p: 227
Alderley, Ches, church 158
    incumbent of see Stanley, M. Richard
Aleyn, Thomas. incumbent of
    Handsworth 125
Aleyn, Thomas. r. or warden of Cresswell
    chapel a: 227, s: 230, d: 232, p: 233
Aleyn, William. incumbent of
    Baxterley 11

Alstone [Alverton], Staffs, vicarage 102
    vicar of see Mason, William
Alvaston [Aylewaston], Derb,
    vicarage 69
    vicars of see Derby, br. William;
    Fissher, Robert
Anston, Thomas. chantry pt. of mediety
    of Percy chantry in Holy Trinity,
    Coventry 61
Appleby [Appulby], unidentified, Thomas
    del Astley of, q.v.
appropriation xi
Arbury [Erbury, Erdebury], Warw, prior
    and convent of 3, 36
    canons of see Gloucestre, Richard;
    Rugeley, Thomas; Shiplond, Richard
    ordinand to title of see Betteley,
    Thomas
Ardeweke, Roger d: 219, p: 220
Arnall, br. John s: 221
Arundel, lord see Arundell, John
Arundell, John, lord Arundel and
    Mautravers 131
Ashby, Canons [Assheby], Northants,
    ordinand to title of see Hosier,
    Robert
Ashover [Asshoe], Derb, church 65
    incumbent of see Reresby,
    William
Ashton on Mersey [Assheton super
    Mersee], Ches, rectory 180–1

Ashton on Mersey – *contd.*
    rectors of   *see* Bagelegh, William;
        Lytster, Robert
Ask, Roger   115, 117
Asshebery, William. r. Morton, master of
    Sibthorpe college   82–4
Asshebourne, br. Henry. monk of
    Burton   s: 219, d: 220, p: 233
Assheby, Richard. v. Leek Wootton   22
Assheby, William son of Richard de.
        v. Leek Wootton   46
Assheton, John   a: 226, s: 227, d: 230,
        p: 231
Assheton, Richard del, esq.   180
Assheton, Thomas son of John de,
        knt.   189
Assheton, William de   161
Asteley   *see* Astley
Astley [Asteley], Warw, collegiate church,
        dean of 43, 53   *see also* Maryot,
        John; Wildebore, Nicholas
    prebends in   *see* Astley, Wolvey;
        Milverton
    prebendal priests of   *see* Clement,
        William; West, John
    prebendaries of   *see* Cristenmasse, M.
        Thomas; Howbell, M. John
    lord of   *see* Astley, William de
Astley, Wolvey [Wolvey Asteley], Warw,
        prebend in Astley church, prebendary
        of   *see* Howbell, M. John
    priest of   *see* Clement, William; West,
        John
Astley (Asteley), Giles   a: 221, s: 226,
        d: 227, p: 228
Astley, John   a: 237
Astley, Thomas del, of Appleby   11
Astley, Thomas. lord of Hillmorton   58
Astley, William de. lord of Astley   42, 56
Aston, br. John, monk of Shrewsbury
        s: 219, d: 224, p: 236
Atherston, br. John, monk of
        Merevale   p: 219
Atherstone [Atherston], Warw, Austin
        friars of   *see* Ayleward, John; Barowe,
        John; Borgh, John; Peynter, John;
        Mustelwike, William; Vernon, Henry
Attingham [Attyngham], Warw,
        vicarage   139
    vicar of   *see* Weston, Richard
Aughton [Aghton], Lancs,
        rectory   163–4

rectors of   *see* Bradschagh, John de;
    Spynk, John
Augustinian friars, houses of
        see Atherstone, Stafford,
    Warrington
Austrey, Warw, church of   xi
Averay, Roger   a: 236
Ault Hucknall   *see* Hucknall, Ault
Aumale [Albemalie], earl of
        see Clarence, duke of
Avon Dassett [Aven Dorset, Avendorset],
        Warw, rectory   12–14
    rectors of   *see* Benet, Alexander;
        Excetre, John
Axholme [Axiholm], Lincs, Carthusian
        house at   49, 63
Ayleward (Aylleward), br. John, O.S.A.,
        of Atherstone   d: 231, p: 233

Babthorp, Robert, knt.   158
Baddesley Clinton [Baddesley], Warw,
        church   47
    incumbent of   *see* West, John
    lady of   *see* Burdet, Joan.
Bagelegh (Baggelegh), William. r. Ashton
        on Mersey, r. Wistaston   180–1
Baker, Robert   a: 233, s: 238
Baker, Roger   s: 221, d: 222, p: 224
Baker, Thomas   a: 234
Bamburgh, Robert son of Simon de (once
        Simon). r. Little Gidding, r.
        Dalbury   74–5
    see also Bilburgh
Bangor, Wales, bp. of   *see* Barrow, William
Bangor Iscoed [Bangore], Flint,
        rectory   167
    rectors of   *see* Leyot, M. John;
        Straunge, John
Barbot, Thomas   a: 240
Barbour, M. John. notary public   185,
        215, 217
Barnvil, br. Richard   a: 242
Baro, Richard. v. Barrow upon Trent   88
Barowe, br. John, O.S.A., of
        Atherstone   s: 233
Barrow, William. bp. Bangor, vicar
        general for bp. of London   177–8
    seal of, as vicar general   177
Barrow upon Trent [Barowe super Trent],
        Derb, vicar of   *see* Baro, Richard
Bartlot, William. v. Willoughby   45
    Barton, Robert   a: 234

Barton, Robert, dioc. Lincoln   s: 234,
　　d: 235, p: 236
Barton, M. Thomas. Treasurer of
　　Lichfield   185
Baschurch [Bassechirche, Bassechurch],
　　Salop, vicarage of   145–7, 151–3
　　vicars of   see Bouch, M. John; Pole,
　　John; Wicherley, Thomas
Basingwerk [Basyngwerk, Basyngwerke],
　　Flint, abbot and convent of   66
　　ordinand to title of   see Clyff, Thomas
Basset, Edmund, esq.   116
bastardy   see dispensations
Baswich, Staffs, canons of   see Broghton,
　　Adam; Colman, Richard; Morton,
　　John
　　ordinands to title of   see Clerc, Roger;
　　Wymark, John
Bate, Laurence   a: 242
Batman, Thomas   a: 239
Baxster, Ralph   p: 219
Baxster, Thomas. chantry pt. in
　　Huyton   161
Baxterley, Warw, church of   11
　　incumbent of   see Aleyn, William
Bayens   see Bayons
Bayly, Roger   a: 243
Bayons (Bayens), John   4, 6
Beauchief [Bello Capite], Derb, canons
　　of   see Fereby, John; Fox, Roger;
　　Selby, John
　　ordinand to title of   see Brome, William
Beaufort, Henry. bp. of Winchester. vicar
　　general for   see Forest, John
Beche, William   a: 239
Bedworth, Warw, chapel of St Mary,
　　chantry in   3, 36
　　pt. of   see Clare, Richard; Longlee,
　　John
Bee, Richard   s: 242, d: 243, p: 244
Begon, William. r. Bradley, prebendal
　　v. Fridaythorpe   81
Belamy, John   a: 236, s: 237, d: 238,
　　p: 239
Bele, Richard. warden of Salbourne
　　chapel   s: 227
Bele, William   a: 237
Belington, John (?same as John
　　Welinton)   d: 239, p: 242
Belle, Richard   a: 241
Benet, Alexander. r. Avon Dassett,
　　r. Fenny Drayton   12–14

Berdemore, Hugh   a: 243
Bereford, Elizabeth, widow of Baldwin   21
Beriton   see Bertton
Bernard, M. John. r. Wappenbury   49
Berrington [Biryton], Salop, church   148
　　incumbent of   see Gomond, John
Bertem (Bertrem), Thomas   s: 221,
　　d: 222, p: 224
Bertton (Briton, Beriton), William
　　s: 232, d: 233, p: 234
Besevile, M. John. r. Southam   32
Beston (Beyston), br. William. canon of
　　Lilleshall   s: 236, d: 242
Betons Ithell, dioc. St David's, r. of
　　see Legburn, William
Betteley, Thomas   s: 239
Beuglegh, Richard   s: 221, d: 222
Bewford, John   p: 219
Beyston   see Beston
Bicester [Burcestre], Oxon, prior and
　　convent of   27, 29
Bickenhill [Bikenhull, Bykenhull], Warw,
　　vicarage   18–20
　　vicars of   see Bikenhill, William;
　　Croxale, Nicholas de
Bikenhill (Bikenhull, Bikkenhill,
　　Bikkenhull), John   s: 239, d: 242,
　　p: 243
Bikenhill, William. v. Bickenhill, r.
　　Saxby   18–20
Bilburgh (Bamburgh, Bilbourgh), Henry
　　de. r. Boyleston, r. mediety of East
　　Keal   91–3
Birdingbury [Birdyngesbury, Briddyngbury,
　　Brydyngbury, Byrdyngbury], Warw,
　　rector of   see Bradwell, John
Birkenhead [Birkehed, Birkhed], Ches,
　　monk of   see Goldyng, Samson
　　ordinands to title of   see Blene,
　　Gilbert; Bonell, Thomas; Grenehode,
　　John/Richard; Molynton, John;
　　Roby, John; Smyth, Adam; Sonky,
　　Robert; Stanley, Ralph/Ranulf;
　　Swynley, Robert; Wodehous, John;
　　Wodelok, John; Wolaston, Richard
Birmingham [Birmyncham, Birmyngham],
　　Warw, hospital of St Thomas the
　　Martyr   30
　　master of   see Prestwode, William
Biscathorpe [Bisshopethorp,
　　Bisshopthorp], Lincs, rector of
　　see West, John

Bishops Hatfield *see* Hatfield, Bishops
Bishops Itchington *see* Itchington,
Bishops
Blakelowe, Robert p: 219
Blakeway (Blakewey), br. John. monk of
Buildwas s: 227, d: 237, p: 239
Blene, Gilbert d: 234, p: 236
Blevyn, Gilbert (?same as preceding)
a: 231
Blomer, John. incumbent of
Cheadle 168
Blondell (Blundell), Robert s: 238,
d: 239, p: 240
Blore, Staffs, rectory 115–116
rectors of *see* Halom, Robert; Lowthe,
John de
Blowdon, John s: 230, d: 231, p: 232
Blundell *see* Blondell
Bobenhull, prebend in Lichfield
cathedral xi, 218
prebendaries of *see* Goldeston,
William; Parys, M. Maior
Body, Edward. incumbent of
Hampton 142
Boidell *see* Boydell
Bokelond (Bukland), William a: 240;
s: 244
Bolde, William a: 232
Bolde, M. William, LL.B. (?same as
preceding) s: 239, d: 240, p: 241
Boleton (Bulton), br. John. canon of
Darley s: 231, d: 236
Bolton, Henry de a: 236, s: 237, d: 238,
p: 239
Bologna, Italy ix
Bolton, Thomas s: 237, d: 238, p: 239
Bone, John s: 244
Bonell, Thomas s: 239, d: 240, p: 241
Bonyngton, John a: 224
books, theft of 200
Bordesley, Worcs, ordinand to title of
see Lyne, Robert
Borgh (Borowe), br. John, O.S.A., of
Atherstone d: 240, p: 242
Borun (Burton), Elizabeth daughter of
John, knt. 189
Alice, sister of 189
Bosedon, John s: 238, d: 239, p: 242
Boseley, Geoffrey de. claimant to rectory
of Wilmslow 182–3
Boseworth (Bosworth), William s: 224,
d: 225, p: 226

Bosvyle *see* Bosvyll
Bosvyll (Bosevile, Bosvyle), Richard
s: 242, d: 243, p: 244
Bosworth *see* Boseworth
Bote, John. chantry pt. in St Michael
Cornhill, London; r.
Stockton 38–40
Boteler, Andrew, knt. 177, 179
Boteler, Philip, knt. lord of Norbury 111
Bothe, Robert del, esq. 182–3
Bothe, William de. r. Wilmslow 166
Boton, John 124
Botyler, Thomas. v. Harbury 24
Bouch (Bouche), M. John. v. Baschurch,
r. Llanfachairn, r. mediety of
Walton 145–7, 151–3
Bourgh (Burgh), br. Richard. monk of
Whalley p: 224
Bourgh, br. Thomas. monk of Combe
s: 231, d: 236, p: 239
Bowell, br. William, O.F.M., of
Lichfield a: 226, s: 227, d: 228,
p: 243
Bower *see* Bowher
Bowet, Henry, abp. of York 82, 85, 115
Bowher (Bower), Roger s: 221, d: 230,
p: 237
Bowland (Bowlond), Robert d: 219, p: 220
Boydell (Boidell), Henry. r. Standon
d: 237, p: 239
Boydell, John, esq., proctor for Nicholas
Crosseby 37
Boyleston [Boileston], Derb,
rectory 91–2
rectors of *see* Bilburgh, Henry de;
Germethorpe, Robert de
Boys, John, jr., esq. 177, 179
Brabson, Richard s: 231, d: 232 (?see
also Braybon)
Brabson, Thomas s: 231, d: 232, p: 233
Bradesale (Bradeshall), br. Thomas, canon
of Darley s: 231, d: 236
Bradkirke, br. Edward, O.F.M., of
Lichfield a: 226, s: 238
Bradley, Derb, rectory xii, 78–9, 81
rectors of *see* Begon, William; Fouler,
John; Fridaythorp alias Clerk, John
Bradney, William s: 243, d: 244
Bradschagh (Bradschawe), John de. r.
Aughton, r. Freshwater 163–5
Bradschagh, Roger de, esq. 108
Matilda, late wife of 164

Bradschagh, Roger de, esq., lord of
Meynell Langley, ordinand to title of
see Bee, Richard
Bradwell, John. r. Birdingbury a: 224,
s: 225, d: 226, p: 227
Brailsford [Braylesford], Derb, church 77
incumbent of *see* Pole, M. John
Brampton, Simon. bp.
Tripolitanensis 220–5
Braybon, Laurence a: 233, s: 234,
d: 236, p: 237
Braybon, Richard p: 233 (?same as
Richard Brabson)
Braynoke (Breynok), br. Richard. monk of
St Anne near Coventry s: 236,
d: 237, p: 238
Breadsall Park [Bradeshaleparke,
Bradeshallpark, Bradeshallparke,
Bradeshall Parke], Derb, canon
of *see* Holand, Thomas
ordinands to title of *see* Tailour, John;
Wade, Thomas
Bredon, br. John. canon of Church
Gresley s: 221, d: 222, p: 237
Brendurgas, br. Ed., O.F.M., of
Lichfield d: 237
Brereton, Aleysa, widow of William
de xi
husband of *see* Holes, Thomas
Bresty, John, esq. 181
Bretton, Monk [Monkebreton], Yorks,
ordinand to title of *see* Wordworth,
William
Brewood [Brewod], Staffs, White nuns.
prioress and convent of 140, 143
Breynok *see* Braynoke
Brid (Bridde), James a: 230, s: 231,
d: 232, p: 233
Bridgnorth [Brugenorth, Brugenorthe,
Bruggenorth], Salop, hospital of St
James, ordinands to title of
see Cardemaker, William; Erkale,
Thomas; Felelot, Thomas; Gratsford,
William; Howell, Thomas; Robyns,
John; Robyns, Thomas; Rusheton,
Richard; Warde, Edward
Bristowe, br. Thomas, O.Carm., of
Coventry a: 225
Briton *see* Bertton
Brodey, Walter a: 227
Broghton, br. Adam. canon of
Baswich p: 219

Brome, William s: 221, d: 222, p: 224
Bromeley (Bromley), br. John. canon of
Rocester s: 233, d: 237
Brompston, br. John. lieutenant of br.
William Hulles, prior of the Order of
St John of Jerusalem in England 91,
93
Brompton (Bromton), br. Robert. canon
of Rocester s: 232, d: 233, p: 234
Bromwich, br. Thomas, O.F.M., of
Lichfield d. 238, p: 239
Broun, Adam a: 237
Broun, Henry s: 226, d: 227, p: 230
Broun, John a: 221
Broun, John a: 226
Broun, John s: 227, d: 228
Broun, John s: 236, d: 237, p: 239
Broun, Walter a: 242
Bruton, M. Richard. chancellor of Wells,
vicar general of the bp. of
London 38–9
Bruyne (Bryne), John a: 221
Bruyne, William a: 231, s: 232, d: 233,
p: 234
Bubton *see* Bukton
Buckingham [Buckyngham], Bucks,
archdeacon of 151, 153
Official of 151, 153
Bucley (Bulcley, Bulkeley), Isabella 193
husband of *see* Butterworth, William
son of John de
Buildwas [Bildewas, Buldewas], Salop,
monk of *see* Blakeway, John
ordinands to title of *see* Bradney,
William; Hechecok, John; Ustanes,
William
Bukland *see* Bokelond
Bukton (Bubton), Thomas 4, 6
Bul, Richard. incumbent of
Tattenhall 162
Bulcley, Bulkeley *see* Bucley
Bullok, M. Walter, canon of Lichfield,
vicar general for bishop
Catterick ix–xi, 1–218, *passim*
keeper of spiritualities of Lichfield, *sede
vacante* x–xi
register of, as vicar general ix–xii
Bulton *see* Boleton
Burdet, Joan. lady of Baddesley 47
Burgeys (Burges), br. Walter, O.F.M.
s: 226, d: 227
Burgh *see* Bourgh

Burghill, John. bp. of Coventry and
Lichfield ix
register of x
Burnell, Hugh, knt. lord of Holdgate and
Weoley 109, 127
Burnell, br. Richard. canon of
Haughmond s: 219, d: 224, d: 231
(properly p.)
Burscogh, br. Nicholas. monk of
Upholland s: 236, d: 238, p: 243
Burscough [Bourscogh, Burscogh], Lancs,
ordinands to title of see Ardeweke,
Roger; Blondell, Robert; Broun,
Henry; Corker, Robert; Cosyn,
Richard; Haysnap, William;
Kelcheth, Matthew de; Kirkcorms,
John; Lancelyn, Robert; Lawe, John;
Loweles, William; Mos, Richard;
Shirwalacres, Henry; Smyth,
William; Stanyhurst, Thomas;
Sutton, Henry; Tarlton, Reginald de;
Tildesley, Ranulf de; Toppyng,
Henry; Wall, Nicholas; Walton,
Richard; Wolfall, Nicholas
Burton on Trent [Burton, Burton super
Trent], Staffs, abbot and convent
of xi, 106
monks of see Asshebourne,
Henry; More, Thomas; Norton,
Thomas; Richard; Warde,
Nicholas
ordinands to title of see Clerc,
Henry; Shyngler, Thomas;
Steyn, Thomas
document dated at xi
Burton, John, clk. proctor for Robert
Thresk 51
Burton, John, of Copeland 201
Burton, br. John. canon of Church
Gresley a: 221, s: 222, d: 223, p: 225
Burton, br. Robert, O.P., of Warwick
a: 242
Burton see also Borun
Busch, John d: 219
Buscy, John, knt. 83
Bussy, John, knt. lord of Hougham 72
Butterworth (Butterley, Butturworth),
William son of John de 193, 197
wife of see Bucley, Isabella

Cadeby, Lincs, chapel see Wyham
college

Canons Ashby see Ashby, Canons
Canterbury, abp. of see Chichele, Henry
Canwell [Canwall], Staffs, ordinand to
title of see Elmeton, Robert
Cardemaker, William a: 241, s: 242,
d: 243, p: 244
Carix, Reginald. v. Offchurch,
v. Wolfhamcote 7, 8, 25
Carlisle, bp. of see Strickland, William
Carmelite (no house given)
see Langford, Richard
Carmelite house see Coventry
Carpenter, Hugh. chantry pt. in Enville
church 123
Carter, Roger a: 239
Carthusians, houses of see Axholme,
Coventry, Sheen
Castle Rising [Castell Risyng,
Castelrisyng], Norf, rector of
see Elleswike, John
Catesby, John, esq. 44
Catesby, Northants, ordinands to title
of see Hore, William; Schagh,
Ralph
Catterick [Catrik, Katrik], John. bp. of
Coventry and Lichfield, bp. of
Exeter 122
career of ix
lodgings of, in Geneva 122
register of ix–xii
unregistered acts of xi – xii
vicar general of see Bullok, Walter
commissary of see Norton, John
commission to 1
Catterick, Robert. canon of Lichfield;
dean of St Chad, Shrewsbury a and
s: 225
Catysby, br. William, O.P. d: 226
Caudray, William. monk of
Stoneleigh d: 236
Cave, William de. chantry pt. in Huyton
church 161
Caverswall [Careswall], Staffs,
vicarage 126
vicars of see Coltan, John; Person,
William
Cawood [Cawod, Cawode], Yorks,
documents dated at 82, 85, 115
Cay, Thomas d: 235, p: 236
Chaddesden, Derb, chantry in chapel of,
second chaplaincy of 100
chaplain of see Shardelowe, Geoffrey

Chadwike, Chadwyk   see Chedwike
Charley [Cherley, Cherleya], Leics, monks
    of 188 see also Loghtborowe, John
    ordinand to title of   see Derby,
    Nicholas
    prior of, Robert, and kinsmen 188
Chatburn, br. Nicholas s: 242
Chaworth, Thomas, knt. 18, 20
Cheadle [Chedle], Ches, church 168
    incumbent of   see Blomer, John
Checkley [Chekley], Ches, rectory 119
    rector of   see Savage, Thomas
Chedle   see Chell
Chedwike (Chadwike, Chadwyk),
    John   a: 242, s: 243, d: 244
Chell (Chedle), br. John. monk of
    Hulton   a: 227, s: 228, p: 230
Chernok, Ralph alias Houkyn de 217
    wife of   see Radeclif, Alice de
Chester [Cestr'], Ches, archdeaconry.
    archdeacon of 201
    institutions in   154–82
    churches. Holy Trinity, image of Holy
    Trinity in 201
      St John. prebend in 169;
        prebendaries of   see Frysby,
        Richard; Walton, M. Thomas;
        vicar in   see Mason, Ranulf
    documents dated at 183–4
    mayor and sheriff of 201
    religious houses. St Mary, ordinand to
      title of   see Baker, Roger
        St Werburga. abbot of   see
        zerdley, Thomas; abbot and
        convent of 155, 160, 162, 171,
        174, 178; ordinands to title
        of   see Bruyne, William; Coton,
        Thomas de; Lee, Richard de;
        Overton, David de; Sotheworth,
        John
    royal court at 182–3, 201
    justice of   see Holt, James del
Chesterfield [Chesterfeld], Derb,
    document dated at 96
Chichele, Henry. abp. of Canterbury x
    register of xi
Childe (Chylde), Robert   a: 221, s: 224,
    d: 225, p: 226
Chirbury, William. chaplain of
    Rodington 137
Cholmeley, Thomas   a: 232, s: 233,
    d: 234, p: 235

Church Gresley   see Gresley, Church
Church Lawford   see Lawford, Church
Chylde   see Childe
Clare, Richard. chantry pt. at
    Bedworth 3
Clarence, Thomas, duke of; steward of
    England; earl of Aumale 130, 132
Clattercote [Clatercote], Oxon, ordinand
    to title of   see Bikenhill, John
Claxton, William   a: 236
Claybrok (Claybroke), Richard   a: 228,
    s: 229, d: 230, p: 231
Claydon, Edward   a: 239
Clayton, Henry. r. Northmoor   a and
    s: 240; d: 242
Clayton, William 216
Clayton, William   s: 242 (?same as
    above)
Clayton, William   d: 243 (?same as
    above)
Clement VI, pope 204
Clement, William. prebendal pt. of
    Wolvey Astley in Astley church 53
Clerc (Clerk), Henry. a: 221, s: 222,
    d: 224, p: 225
Clerc, Roger   a: 224, s: 226, d: 227,
    p: 228
Clerc, William. r. Wishaw,
    v. Hathersage 21
Clerc, William   d: 219, p: 220
Clerc   see also Fridaythorp
Clerk   see Clerc, Fridaythorp
clerks, criminous 200–1
Cleydon, br. John   a: 239
Cliffe   see Clyff
Clifford, Richard, bp. of London, vicar
    general of   see Barrow, William;
    Bruton, M. Richard
Clifton   see Clyfton
Clifton Campville [Clifton Campvyle,
    Clifton de Campvile, Clyfton (. . .)],
    Staffs, lord of   see Stafford, Edmund
    rectory 103
      rectors of   see Haukyn, Laurence:
      Stafford, M. John
Clifton on Dunsmore [Clyfton, Clyfton
    super Dinnsmore], Warw,
    vicarage 9, 54
      vicars of   see Pent, Robert; Sherman,
      Alexander; Smyth, William;
      Whatton, John
Clopton, William, esq 177, 179

cloths, theft of 200
Clowne [Cloune], Derb, church 95
    incumbent of *see* Morton, Roger
Clyderowe (Clydirowe), br. Ralph. monk
    of Whalley s: 224, d: 230, p: 231
Clyff (Cliffe), Thomas a: 243, s: 244
Clyfton (Clifton), John a: 226
Clyfton, br. Thomas. canon of Church
    Gresley a: 238, s: 239, d: 240, p: 241
Clyfton, br. Thomas s: 244
Clyfton, William. v. Stoneleigh 35
Clyfton, William s: 227, d: 228, p: 229
Clynton, Elizabeth de 30
Cockersand [Kokirsand], Lancs, ordinand
    to title of *see* Coton, M. John
Coddington [Codyngton], Ches,
    rectory 155
    rectors of *see* Holbroke, John; Potter,
    Nicholas
Coke, Henry a: 230, s: 232, d: 233, p: 234
Coke, John a: 238
Coleshill [Colshill], Warw, lord of
    see Monford, William
collation to benefices 122, 147, 169
Colman, br. Richard. canon of Baswich.
    a:221, s: 230, d:236
Colonia, br. Antony de, O.F.M., of
    Lichfield d: 226
Colonia, br. Henry de, O.F.M., of
    Lichfield s: 227, d: 228
Colonia, br. Sibertus de, O.F.M., of
    Lichfield d: 226
Coltan, John. v. Caverswall,
    v. Dilhorne 126
Combe [Comba, Cumba], Warw, monks
    of *see* Bourgh, Thomas: Coventre,
    John; Sharp, Stephen
    ordinand to title of *see* Fissher, John
Combermere [Cumbermere], Ches, monks
    of *see* Acton, William; Hewster,
    Roger
    ordinands to title of *see* Bokelond,
    William; Cholmeley, Thomas
commissions. appointing vicar general 1
    to admit and install prebendary 218
    to exchange benefices 4, 12, 15, 18,
    23, 27, 50, 55, 74, 78, 81–2, 85, 91,
    107, 115, 130, 145, 151, 163, 169,
    177
commissions, from papal penitentiary, to
    process dispensations
    see dispensations

Concordia, Italy, bp. of *see* Ponte,
    Antony de
Conede, Thomas. incumbent of
    Pitchford 127
consanguinity *see* dispensations
Constance, Germany. Council of ix
    documents dated at xi, 186, 188–94,
    198–9, 202–4, 210–11
Copeland [Copelond], Lancs, John Burton
    of q.v.
Coppe, William, of Coventry 59
Coppenall, Thomas. r. Woodchurch 175
Corker, Robert p: 219
Corley, William. prebendal v. Prees,
    r. Forton 109–10
Cosyn, Richard a: 238, s: 239, d: 240,
    p: 242
Coton, John, of Ridware 92
Coton, M. John, LL.B. d: 237, p: 238
Coton, Thomas de a: 229, s: 236, s: 237
    (properly d), p: 238
Coton, br. William. canon of Norton.
    d: 231 (properly s); d: 233, p: 238
Coudray, br. William. monk of
    Stoneleigh d: 225
Cound [Conde], Salop, rectory 130–1,
    135
    rectors of *see* Osbarn, John: Wyndhill,
    John
Coventre, br. John. monk of Combe
    p: 231
Coventre, John de s: 237, d: 238, p: 239
Coventry [Coventr'], Warw,
    archdeaconry, institutions in 2–63
    Carmelites of *see* Abyndon, John;
    Bristowe, Thomas; Hampton, Henry;
    Langford, William; Newson, John;
    Spyne, Robert; Stanton, Robert;
    Stavnford, John
    Carthusian house of St Anne near,
    monk of *see* Braynoke, Richard
    prior and convent of 26
    cathedral. monks of *see* London,
    Thomas; Northampton, John;
    Pollesworth, Thomas
    ordination in 225
    prior of *see* Crosseby, Richard
    prior and convent of 7, 37, 51, 62
    churches
    Holy Trinity, mediety of Percy
    chantry in 61; priest of *see*
    Anston, Thomas; Fawcus, Robert

St Michael, vicarage   50–2, 62;
    vicars of   *see* Glymme, M.
    William; Leyot, M. Richard;
    Thresk, Robert de
documents dated at   32, 65, 107
hospital of St John, ordinands to title
    of   *see* Asteley, Giles; Forst, Roger;
    Gerard, John; Hachet, William; Ive,
    William; Loxley, Thomas; Nowell,
    John; Robyns, John; Smyth, Thomas;
    Waren, Richard; Wer, Thomas atte;
    Westley, John
Cowley, Thomas   a: 231, s: 232, d: 233,
    p: 234
Cranley, Thomas, LL.B. r. Bishops
    Hatfield, commissary and lieutenant
    of abp. of Dublin in royal free chapel
    of Penkridge   107
Cranley, Thomas. abp. Dublin, primate of
    Ireland, dean of royal free chapel of
    Penkridge   107
commissary of   *see* Cranley, Thomas
Cressewell (Cressale, Cressall), br. John,
    O.S.A., of Warrington   s: 236,
    d: 237, p: 238
Cresswell [Cressewell, Cressewall,
    Cresswall], Staffs, thefts at   200
Cresswell, Staffs/Derb, chapel, warden
    of   *see* Aleyn, Thomas
Crich, Derb, vicarage   98
  vicars of   *see* Penyale, Hugh; Trusbut,
    Peter
Christenmasse, M. Thomas, B.Theol.
    prebendary of Milverton in Astley
    church   42
Cronage (Croneegge), Thomas   a: 229,
    s: 239, d:240, p: 241
Crosseby, Nicholas. prebendary of Ufton
    Cantoris   37
  proctor of   *see* Boidell, John
Crosseby, br. Richard. prior of
    Coventry   61
Crossepeny, John   s: 243, d: 244
Croston, Lancs, church
    170
  incumbent of   *see* Fyssheburn, Thomas
Crowland, Lincs, ordinand to title of
    see Clayton, William
Croxale (Croxhale), Nicholas de.
    v. Bickenhill, r. Saxby   18–20
Croxden [Crokesden], Staffs, abbot and
    convent of   102

monk of   *see* Leylond, Ralph
  ordinand to title of   *see* Wetrev, Hugh
Croxhale   *see* Croxale
Croxton [Crokesden], Leics, abbot and
    convent of   101
Crukadam (Crukeadam), M. Geoffrey.
    canon of Salisbury; vicar general of
    Salisbury   130–1
Cuckow Church [Cokkochurch], Warw,
    rector of   *see* Verney, John.
Curson, John, esq.   73
Curson, Thomas. r. Pipewell   d: 244
Curteys, Robert   a: 242

Daa, Thomas   a: 227
Dalbury, Derb, rectory   74–5
  rectors of   *see* Bamburgh, Robert son of
    Simon de; Toneworth, William
Dale [Dala], Derb, abbot and convent
    of   97, 99
  canons of   *see* Derby, Thomas; Dufield,
    John; Sutton, Henry
  ordinands to title of   *see* Bertrem,
    Thomas; Bowher, Roger; Elyot, John;
    Hill, Nicholas; Kirkeby, Thomas;
    Sandiaker, William
Dalton, br. Richard, O.S.A., of
    Stafford   s: 230
Dalton, br. Richard, of Warrington (same
    as above?)   d: 231, p: 232
Danby, John   a: 232
Darlaston [Dorlaston], Staffs,
    rectory   112
  rector of   *see* Jamiesson, William
Darley [Derle, Derley], Derb, abbot and
    convent of   64, 98, 100
  canons of   *see* Boleton, John;
    Bradesale, Thomas; Grene, Thomas
  ordinands to title of   *see* Hervy,
    Richard; Kyngeston, John; Scaumsby,
    Thomas
Dauntre, Thomas. incumbent of
    Swarkeston   89
Davenham, Ches, church   176
  incumbent of   *see* Holes, Andrew
Davers, William   a: 233
Dawes, William   d: 219, p: 221
Dawkyn, John   a: 236
Dedyk, John   118
  Margaret, wife of   118
Denton, br. Henry, O.F.M., of
    Lichfield   p: 231

Derby [Derbeye], Derb, archdeaconry of,
    institutions to benefices in   64–101
  documents dated at   69
  nunnery near   see Kings Mead
Derby, Nicholas   s: 244
Derby, br. Thomas. canon of Dale   p: 226
Derby, br. William. v. Alvaston   69
Desford (Dysford), br. John, O.S.A., of
    Stafford   a: 230, s: 232, d: 233,
    p: 234
Deyncourt, Alice   71
Deyne, br. John   s: 244
Dichefeld, Thomas   s: 237, d: 238, p: 239
Dieulacres [Dieulaucres, Dieulecresse,
    Dieuleucres], Staffs, abbot and
    convent of   172
  monks of   see Godefelowe, John;
    Henschawe, John
  ordinands to title of   see Assheton,
    John; Bosedon, John; Prestbury,
    William de
Dilhorne [Dolver (. . .), Dulvern,
    Dulverne], Staffs, vicarage   104, 126
  vicars of   see Coltan, John; Person,
    William
dispensations. for bastardy   190–1,
    195–6, 198, 205–8, 210–16
  from irregularity   188, 199
  to confirm marriage   xi, 192, 194, 202
  to permit marriage   186, 189, 193,
    197, 203–4, 217
Dobnam, br. John de. monk of
    Whalley   p: 224
Dominicans (no house given)
    see Catysby, William; Heyne, William
Dominican houses   see Leicester,
    Newcastle under Lyme,
    Northampton, Shrewsbury, Stafford,
    Warwick
Don, John. v. Stanton upon Hine
    Heath   144
Donington [Donyngton], Salop,
    church   136
  incumbent of   see Hody, M. John
Dorchester [Dircacestre, Dorcacestre,
    Dorcascestre], Oxon, ordinand to
    title of   see Lyne, Richard
Dore, Heref, abbot and convent of   149
Dorlaston, Thomas de   112
Draycote, Roger   a: 236
Drayton, Fenny [Fennydrayton,
    Fenydrayton], Leics, rectory   12–14

rectors of   see Benet, Alexander;
    Excetre, John
Drayton, Market [Drayton in Hales],
    Salop, vicarage   128, 134
  vicars of   see Falk, Henry; Walbron,
    John
Drayton, Thomas   a: 232, s: 233, d: 235,
    p: 236
Dublin, Ireland, abp. of   see Cranley,
    Thomas
Duffeld (Duffield), br. John. canon of
    Dale   s: 226, d: 227
Duffeld, M. Robert. notary public   185,
    215
Duffeld, M. Thomas. chancellor of
    Lincoln cathedral and prebendary of
    Sutton   78, 80
Duffelt, John. v. Loppington   129
Duffield   see Duffeld
Dugdale, Richard   s: 242, d: 243, p: 244
Duncalf, John. v. Prestbury   160
Dunvile (Dunvyle), Roger. r. of mediety of
    Lymm   156, s: 224
Durham. bp. of   see Langley, Thomas
  diocese, ordinand from   see Swynburn,
    Thomas
Dysford   see Desford

East Keal   see Keal, East
Eccleshall [Eccleshale], Staffs   200–1
  church. ordination in   229
      purgation of criminous clerks
    in   200–1
  prebendal vicarage of   120
    vicar of   see Neweport, M.
    Gregory
  prebendary of   see Bullok, M. Walter
  vicar of   see Norton, John
Egerton, ?Ches, John Philippi of, q.v.
Ellesmer, Roger. v. Loppington   129
Ellesmere [Ellesmer], Salop, lord of
    see Lestraunge, Richard
Elleswike (Elswike), John. r. Castle
    Rising   d: 238, p: 242
Elmdon [Elmedon, Elmendon, Elmyndon],
    Warw. lady of   see Waldyns, Joanna
  rectory   23
      rectors of   see Palmer, William;
    Tudde, John
Elmeton, Robert   a: 242, s: 243, d: 244
Elswike   see Elleswike
Elyot, John   a: 233, s: 234, d: 236, p: 237

Elyot, John   a: 233, s: 236, d: 237, p: 238
Elys, Gerard. v. Scarcliff   64
Endon, Roger de   a: 244
England, king of, as duke of
    Lancaster   77, 114, 157
    as patron   105, 124, 135
    [Henry IV], son of   see Clarence, duke
    of
England, Steward of   see Clarence, duke
    of
Enville [Enefeld], Staffs, chantry of the
    Blessed Virgin Mary in the church
    of   123
    priest of   see Carpenter, Hugh
Erdeswik, Samson. r. Kingsley   108
Erkale (Erkalle), Thomas   s: 239, d: 240,
    p: 241
Evston   see Ustanes
Ewell, John   177, 179
Excetre, John. r. Avon Dassett, r. Fenny
    Drayton   12–14
exchanges of benefices.   xi – xii, 4–8,
    12–21, 23, 25, 27–9, 38–40, 50–2,
    55–7, 74–6, 78–87, 91–3, 107,
    109–10, 115–17, 126, 130–2,
    145–7, 151–3, 163–5, 169, 177–81
excommunication   199   see also
    dispensations to confirm marriages
Exeter, bp. of   see Catterick, John;
    Stafford, Edmund
Eyam [Eyom], Derb, church   68
    incumbent of   see Stedman, Roger
Eyre (Eyer), Denise   203
    husband of   see Hall, Thurston de

Fairford, Henry   131
Falk, Henry. v. Market Drayton   128,
    134
Falk, Henry v. Stanton upon Hine
    Heath   144
Falke, Richard   s: 242, d: 243, p: 244
Faryngton, Laurence   s: 239, d: 242,
    p: 243
Fawcus, Roger. pt. of a mediety of the
    Percy chantry in Holy Trinity,
    Coventry   61
Fayrford, Henry. litteratus   217
Feidyn, Geoffrey   a: 232
Felelot (Felilode, Felylode), Thomas
    a: 227, s: 228, d: 229, p: 230
Felley [Felle], Northants, ordinands to title
    of   see Normanton, John; Warde, Ed.

Felton, William. r. Ross Hall   141
Felylode   see Felelot
Fenny Drayton   see Drayton, Fenny
Fere, Adam de   s: 237, d: 238, p: 239
Fereby, br. John. canon of Beauchief
    s: 234
Fissher (Fyssher), James   s: 227, d: 230,
    p: 231
Fissher, John   s: 237, d: 238, p: 239
Fissher, Robert   s: 233
Fissher, Robert (same as above?)   d: 234,
    p: 235
Fissher, Robert. v. Alvaston   69
Fissher, William   s: 220, d: 221, p: 224
Fissher, William   a: 238
Fleccher, John   d: 236, p: 237
Flessher, Thomas. v. Bishops Itchington,
    r. Newton Purcell   27–8
Florence, Italy   ix
    document dated at   216
Flynt, br. Denis   s: 243
Folk, Richard   a: 230
Forberg   see Forbrig
Forbour, M. William. notary public   185
Forbrig (Forberg), br. Laurence,
    O.SA./O.P., of Stafford   s: 237,
    d: 238, p: 239
Ford, Old [Oldeford], Midd, document
    dated at   50
Forest, br. Howell, O.P., of
    Shrewsbury   d: 239
Forest, John. archdeacon of Surrey, canon
    of Lichfield and Lincoln, prebendary
    of Prees, vicar general of
    Winchester   110, 163
Forst, Roger   s: 225, d: 226, p: 227
Forst, Thomas   s: 227, d: 230, p: 231
Forton, Staff, rectory   109
    rectors of   see Admondeston, Thomas:
    Corley, William
Forton, John   a: 241
Fouler, John. r. Bradley, prebendal v.
    Sutton le Marsh   78–80
Fouleshurst, Richard. r. Woodchurch   175
Fouleshurst, Thomas de, esq.   175
Fox, br. Roger. canon of Beauchief
    s: 234, d: 237
Foxton, Leics, Richard Spicer of, q.v.
Frances   see Fraunceys
Franciscans (no house identified)
    see Burgeys, Walter; Horald, John;
    Neston, Thomas.

79

Franciscan houses *see* Lichfield,
Northampton, Nottingham, Oxford
Fraunces (Frances, Fraunceys),
Thomas a: 222, s: 230, d: 231,
p: 232
Freeford, prebend in Lichfield
cathedral x
Freshwater [Freswater], I.O.W.,
rectory 163–5
rectors of *see* Bradschagh, John de;
Spynk, John
Fridaythorp alias Clerk (Clerc), John.
r. Bradley, v. Sutton le Marsh,
v. Fridaythorpe 78–9, 81
Fridaythorpe, Yorks, vicarage 81
prebendal vicars of *see* Begon,
William; Fridaythorp alias Clerk,
John
Frysby (Frisby), Richard. prebendary in St
Mary by the Castle, Leicester;
prebendary in St John, Chester 169
proctor for *see* Temworth, Richard
Fulham, br. Denis s: 244
Fulham, br. John. proctor for Philip
Morgan 157
Fulnetby, John 4, 6
Furnival [Furnyvale], lord *see* Talbot,
John
Fyssheburn, Thomas. incumbent of
Croston 170
Fyssher *see* Fissher
Fytton, Hugh 215
Fytton, M. John. archdeacon of
Stafford 122, 215

Garsyngton, John. v. Willoughby 45
Gaunstede, Ralph de. v. Ilam 106
Gedlyng, Robert a: 237
Geneva, Switzerland, documents dated
at 212–13
lodgings of bp. of Lichfield at 122
Gerard, John a: 238, s: 239, d: 240,
p: 242
Gerard, William a: 238, s: 243, d: 244
Germethorpe (Germethorp), Robert de.
r. Boyleston, r. mediety of East
Keal 91–2
Gerveys, Thomas a: 229
Gibbons (Gybon), John a: 221, s: 222,
d: 224, p: 225
Gidding, Little [Geddyng Parva], Hunts,
rectory 74–6

rectors of *see* Bamburgh, Robert son of
Simon de; Toneworth, William
Glossop [Glossope], Derb, vicarage 66
vicar of *see* Hyndeley, William de
Gloucestre (Glouceter), br. Richard.
canon of Arbury s: 219, d: 237,
p: 238
Glym (Glymme), M. William. v. St
Michael, Coventry; v. St Nicholas,
Newcastle-upon-Tyne 32, 50–2
Godefelowe, br. John. monk of
Dieulacres s: 237
Goldeston, M. William. prebendary of
Bobenhull in Lichfield
cathedral 218
Goldyng, br. Samson. monk of
Birkenhead s: 242
Gomond, John. incumbent of
Berrington 148
Goodman, Roger d: 219
Gracedieu, Leics, ordinands to title
of *see* Barton, Robert; Morgon,
John; Piers, Thomas; Tailour, John;
Thakar, Thomas
Grandborough [Grenebourgh,
Greneburgh], Warw, vicarage 34
vicars of *see* Hildys, John; Screyfeld,
William
Grant, br. William, O.P., of Warwick
a: 242
Grateford, William s: 228, d: 229
Great Packington *see* Packington, Great
Graven (Graver), Cecilia, daughter of
Robert, knt. 192
husbands of *see* Radclif, Ralph son of
Ralph; Venables, Hugh de
Grendon, br. Walter (once John). prior of
St John of Jerusalem in England 74,
76
Grene, br. John. canon of Maxstoke
s: 224, d: 225, p: 231
Grene, br. Thomas. canon of Darley
s: 231, d: 236
Grenehode, John/Richard d: 234, p: 236
Gresley, Church [Grisley, Grisseley],
Derb, canons of *see* Bredon, John;
Burton, John; Clyfton, Thomas;
Melbourne, Robert
ordinands to title of *see* Blowdon,
John; Hunte, William
Grey, Reginald de, lord of Hastings,
Wexford, and Ruthin 151, 153

Grilleshull (Grillushull), Thomas.
v. Wellington 150, 209
Grilleshull, William (once John).
v. Wellington 150, 209
Grossefeld, William p: 219
Gybon see Gibbons
Gybones, Roger. r. mediety of Mugginton,
prebendary in Penkridge chapel
107
Gylot, John. v. Horsley 90

Hachet, William s: 231, d: 232, p: 237
Hadenall (Hodenall), Thomas s: 230,
d: 231, p: 233
Haer see Heyr
Hagno, br. Thomas. canon of
Lilleshall s: 228, d: 237, p: 242
Hailes [Hayles], Glos, ordinands to title
of see Clerc, William; Hurst, John;
Lacheford, Thomas; More, Henry;
Pach, John; Staresmore, Robert;
Tolle, Robert; Warde, Richard
Halle, Thurstan de 203
wife of see Eyre, Denise
Hallum (Halom), Robert. bp. of
Salisbury ix
vicar general of see Crukadam, M.
Geoffrey
Hallum, Robert. r. Blore, r. mediety of
Treswell 115–117
Halughton, Humphrey de, esq. 94
Hamon, Richard. v. Montford 140
Hampton, Salop, chapelry 142
chaplain of see Body, Edward
Hampton, br. Henry (once Richard),
O.Carm., of Coventry s: 225,
d: 230, p: 232
Hanbury [Hambury], Staffs, rectory 114
rector of see Wouburn, John
Hanbury, br. John, canon of Rocester
p: 239
Handley [Hanley], Ches, church 171
incumbent of see Wynwyk,
Richard de
Handsworth [Honnesworth], Staffs,
church 125
incumbent of see Aleyn, Thomas
Hannsard, Richard 4, 6
Hanyngfeld, William, esq. 177, 179
Harborough Magna [Herdeburgh], Warw,
church 41
incumbent of see Smyth, William

Harbury [Herberbury], Warw,
vicarage 24
vicar of see Botyler, Thomas
Harden, Robert p: 219
Harden, br. Thomas de. monk of
Whalley s: 224, d: 230, p: 242
Harley, br. John. canon of Repton
s: 232, d: 233
Harley, William s: 239, d: 242, p: 243
Harpere, John a: 244
Hassale, Thomas. v. Sandbach 172
Hastings [Hastyng], lord of see Grey,
Reginald de
Haston, John 68
Hatfield, Bishops [Hatfield Episcopi],
Herts, rector of see Cranley,
Thomas
Hathersage [Hathersegge], Derb,
vicarage 21
vicars of see Clerc, William; Rolf,
John
Hatton, John 194
wife of see Hycheson, Margaret
Hatton, John s: 221, d: 224, p: 225
Hatton, Laurence de a: 221, s: 222,
d: 224, p: 225
Haughmond [Hagmond, Hamond,
Haugmond], Salop, abbot and
convent of 144
canons of see Burnell, Richard;
Burnell, Richard; Leton, Hugh de;
Leton, Roger; Rissheton, William
ordinands to title of see Koc, John;
Oteley, John
Haukyn, Laurence. r. Clifton
Campville 103
Hawes, br. William s: 244
Haxey, Thomas. lord of Pleasley 96
Haysnap (Haysnape), William a: 227,
s: 232, d: 233, p: 234
Hayward, Richard. v. Wolfhamcote 2
Hayward, Roger. v. Longford 67
Haywood, Staffs, documents dated at xii
Heath [Lound], Derb, vicarage 101
vicar of see Power, Roger
Hechecok, John s: 244
Hechekyn, John a: 236
Hendon, Thomas a: 239
Henschawe, br. John. monk of
Dieulacres s: 237
Henwood [Hynwode], Warw, ordinand to
title of see Hewlot, Thomas

Herby see Hervy
Hereford diocese, ordinands from
    see Grateford, William; Lelye,
    Robert; Longnore, Richard; Lye,
    Roger; Prys, John; Walker, John
Herford, br. Geoffrey, O.P., of
    Northampton d: 239, p: 240
Hert, Richard a: 242
Hertford [Hereford], Herts, prior and
    convent of 39
Hervy (Herby, Herve), Richard a: 236,
    s: 244
Hervy, Richard a: 239, s: 242, d: 243,
    p: 244
Hervy, William. v. Great Packington,
    master of Wyham college with
    Cadeby chapel, v. St Nicholas,
    Leicester 4–6, 15–17
Hesketh, Gilbert de s: 220, d: 221, p: 222
Heton, John de s: 244
Hewlot, Thomas s: 219, d: 220, p: 221
Hewster, br. Roger. monk of
    Combermere s: 226, d: 230
Heyne, br. William, O.P. s: 226
Heyne, William a and s: 241, d: 242
Heyr (Haer), John a: 226, s: 227, d: 228,
    p: 229
Hichons, John a: 221
Hide, Giles a: 232
Hildys, John. v. Grandborough 34
Hill (Hyll), Nicholas d: 221, p: 225
Hill, Robert d: 237, p: 238
Hillmorton [Hillemorton], Warw, church
    of, chantry of St James 59
    priest of see Lye, Philip
    chantry at altar of St Mary 58
    priest of see Tyler, William
    lord of see Astley, Thomas
Hochyn, John s: 237, d: 238, p: 239
Hodenall see Hadenall
Hody, M. John. incumbent of
    Donington 136
Holand, John. chaplain 199
Holand, John son of John, knt. 75
Holand, br. Thomas. canon of Breadsall
    Park s: 233, d: 234, p: 236
Holand, lady see Lovell, Matilda
Holbache, M. Hugh, prebendary of Ufton
    Cantoris in Lichfield cathedral 37
Holbroke, John. r. Coddington 155
Holdgate [Halgot], Salop, lord of
    see Burnell, Hugh

Holes, Andrew. incumbent of
    Davenham 176
Holes, Thomas xi
    Aleysa, wife of xi
Holkote, br. Bartholomew a: 221
Holt, James del. justice of
    Chester 183–4
Holt, br. John, O.F.M., of Lichfield
    a: 222
Honte see Hunte
Horald (Horold), br. John, O.F.M.
    a: 226, s: 227
Hore, William a: 226, s: 242, d: 243,
    p: 244
Horley, William a: 238
Horold see Horald
Horsley, Derb, vicarage 90
    vicars of see Gylot, John; Stacy,
    Thomas
Hosell, Richard. r. Rugby 10
Hosier, Robert s: 219, d: 220, p: 221
Hougham [Hogham], Lincs, lord of
    see Bussy, John
Howard, John, knt. 177, 179
Howbell, M. John. prebendary of Wolvey
    Astley in Astley church 43, 53
Howell, Thomas a: 230, s: 231, d: 232,
    p: 233
Hucknall, Ault [Hegh Hokenall in
    Skaresdale], Derb, vicarage 85–6
    vicars of see Lillyng, Thomas;
    Stapulforth, John
Hule, Thomas s: 244
Hulles, br. William. prior of the Order of
    St John of Jerusalem in England;
    lieutenant for see Brompston, br.
    John
Hulton [Hilton], Staffs, monk of
    see Chell, John
    ordinand to title of see Baxster, Ralph
Hunt see Hunte
Huntar, br. Thomas, O.P., of Warwick
    a: 242
Hunte (Honte, Hunt), br. Walter s: 226
Hunte, William a: 221, s: 222, d: 224,
    p: 225
Hurst, John d: 234, p: 235
Huyton, Lancs, chantry in church 161
    priests of see Baxster, Thomas; Cave,
    William de
Hycheson (Hychonson), Margaret
    daughter of John 194

husband of *see* Hatton, John
  kinswoman of, Alice 194
Hychonson *see* Hycheson
Hyll *see* Hill
Hyndeley, William de. v. Glossop 66
Hynton, John de. master of Sibthorpe
  college, r. Morton 82–3

Idell, William s: 239, d: 242, p: 243
Ideshale, br. Roger. monk of
  Shrewsbury p: 224
Ilam, Staffs, vicarage 106
  vicars of *see* Gaunstede, Ralph de;
  Shirley, Thomas
Ilkeston, Derb, vicarage 97
  vicar of *see* Ilkeston, br. Richard de
Ilkeston, br. Richard de. canon.
  v. Ilkeston 97
inductions to benefices *see* institutions to
  benefices
Inse, William 211
Inse, William. r. Sparham a and s: 237,
  d: 243
institutions to benefices 2–3, 5–11,
  13–14, 16–17, 19–22, 24–6, 28–37,
  39–49, 51–4, 56–73, 75–7, 79–80,
  83–4, 86–90, 92–106, 108–14,
  116–21, 123–9, 131–44, 146,
  148–50, 152–62, 164–8, 170–6,
  178–82
Ipstones (Ipstans), Nicholas a: 233,
  s: 243, d: 244
Ireland, primate of *see* Cranley, Thomas
Iremonger, John. proctor for M. Richard
  Stanley 158
Iremonger, John. v. Walton on the Hill
  (same as above?) 173
irregularity *see* dispensations
Islep, John. v. Bishops Itchington,
  r. Newton Purcell 27–9
Itchington, Bishops [Ichyngton Episcopi],
  Warw, prebendary of *see* Wolden,
  Robert
  vicarage of 27–8
  vicars of *see* Flessher, Thomas; Islep,
  John
Ive, William s: 237, d: 239, p: 242

Jacobi, br. Carmelius, O.F.M., of
  Nottingham d: 239
Jamiesson, William. r. Darlaston 112
Janyn, Stephen a: 244

Jerusalem, order of St John of, priors of in
  England *see* Grendon, Walter;
  Hulles, William
Jervaulx [Gervays], Yorks, ordinand to
  title of *see* Massam, William
Jeykyn, Philip s: 221, d: 222, p: 224
John XXIII, Pope ix
  penitentiary of *see* Orsini, Jordan
John, br., O.F.M., of Nottingham
  p: 236

Katrik *see* Catterick
Keal, East [Esterkele], Lincs, mediety of
  rectory of 91–3
  rectors of *see* Bilburgh, Henry de;
  Germethorpe, Robert de
Kedleston [Kettylleston], Derb,
  rectory 73
  rectors of *see* Leykirke, Walter;
  Whitlombe, Richard
Kefex, Richard s: 220, d: 221, p: 222
Kelcheth, Matthew a: 219, s: 223,
  d: 236, p: 242
Kemsay, William a: 236, s: 237, d: 238,
  p: 239
Kenilworth [Kenilleworth, Kenylleworth,
  Killyngworth], Warw, canons of
  see Napton, Richard; Southam, John;
  Southam, John
  prior and convent of 5, 16, 22, 24, 31,
  35, 46
Kenolmerssh, William 170
Killalo, Ireland, bp. of *see* Mulfield,
  Robert
Killom, Thomas. incumbent of
  Leigh 154
Kilmore, Ireland, bp. of *see* Stockes,
  John
Kings Mead *see* Mead, Kings
Kingsley [Kyngeley], Staffs, rectory 108,
  118
  rector of *see* Erdeswik, Samson;
  Sondon, Nicholas
Kingston Russell [Kyngeston Russell],
  Dors, free chapel 130, 132
  wardens of *see* Osbarn, John;
  Wyndhill, John
Kirk Hallam [Kirkehallum, Kirk Halum],
  Derb, vicarage 99
  vicar of *see* Stonley, br. John
Kirkcorme (Kirkorme), John s: 220,
  d: 221, p: 224

Kirkeby (Kyrkeby), Michael   a: 221
Kirkeby, Thomas   s: 221
Kirkham, br. John   s: 244
Kirkorme   see Kirkcorme
Knaresborough [Knaresborgh,
    Knaresbourgh], Yorks, St Robert,
    ordinand to title of   see Normanton,
    Robert
Knockin [Knokyn], Salop, lord of
    see Lestraunge, Richard
Knyghton, Henry   a: 239
Koc, John   d: 219, p: 220
Kyng, John   s: 238, d: 239, p: 240
Kyng, William   a: 230
Kyngeston, John   s: 227, d: 230, p: 231
Kyrke, John by the. incumbent of Sutton
    Scarsdale   94
Kyrkeby   see Kirkeby
Kyrkeman, Robert. incumbent of North
    Wingfield   71

Lachefer, William. v. Sheriff Hales   113
Lacheford, Thomas   s: 244
Ladbrooke, Warw, church of   xii
Ladyman, Adam   200
Lancaster [Lancastr'], duke of
    see England, king of
Lancaster, Robert. bp. of St
    Asaph   145–7
Lancastreshire (Lancastershire,
    Lancastreshir), Thomas   a: 238,
    s: 240, d: 241, p: 242
Lancelyn (Lanselyn), Robert   a: 237,
    s: 238, p: 240 (?same as Robert
    Lawnlyn)
Lane, John   a: 232
Langford (Lanford, Longford), Iblo.
    r. Nailstone   d: 244
Langford, br. Richard, O.F.M., of
    Northampton   p: 239
Langford, br. Richard, O.Carm   p: 232
    (?same as following)
Langford, br. William, O.Carm., of
    Coventry   s: 226, d: 230
Langford, br. William, O.P., of
    Newcastle   a: 238, s: 239, d: 241
Langley, Meynell [Longley], Derb, lord
    of   see Bradschagh, Roger de
Langley, Thomas. bp. of Durham   50–2
Langnore   see Longnore
Langtre, Ralph de   204
    wife of   see Levelerd, Isabella

Lanselyn   see Lancelyn
Lathum, Nicholas   a: 244
Launde [Landa], Leics, ordinands to title
    of   see Fissher, Robert; Rose, Robert;
    Spencer, Hugh
Lawe, br. Hugh. monk of Vale Royal
    s: 224
Lawe, John   s: 231, d: 232, p: 233
Lawford, Church [Kyrke(. . .)lalleford,
    Kyrkewellaleford], Warw,
    church   26
    incumbent of   see Neweport,
    M. Gregory
Lawnlyn (Lawncelyn), Robert   213
    (?same as Robert Lancelyn)
Lee, br. Henry de. canon of Norton
    d: 231 (properly s.), d: 238
Lee, Richard de   a: 232, s: 233, d: 238,
    p: 242
Leek Wootton [Lekewoton, Lekewotton,
    Lekwotton], Warw, vicarage   22, 46
    vicars of   see Assheby, Richard;
    Assheby, William son of Richard de;
    Racheford, John
Legburghn, William   a: 230 (?same as
    following)
Legburn, William. canon of
    Llandewi-Brefi, r. Betons Ithell
    s: 230, d: 232
Legh, Richard de, esq.   156
Leicester [Leycestr'], Leics. abbey of St
    Mary de Pratis, abbot of
    see Rothley, Richard
    abbot and convent of   9–10, 15, 17, 54
    document dated at   169
    ordinands to title of   see Hochyn, John;
    Wynslowe, Richard
    churches. St Mary by the Castle,
    prebend in   169
        prebendaries of   see Frysby,
        Richard; Walton, M. Thomas
    St Nicholas, vicarage   15, 17
        vicars of   see Hervy, William;
        Shylton, John
    Dominican of   see Swepston, Richard
    hospital of St John, ordinands to title
    of   see Porter, William; Spicer,
    Richard
Leigh [Legh], Lancs, church   154
    incumbent of   see Killom, Thomas
Lelye, Robert   s: 227 (?same as Roger
    Lye)

Lenton, Notts, prior and convent of 90
Lestraunge, Richard. lord of Knockin and
    Ellesmere 142, 167
Leton, br. Hugh de. canon of
    Haughmond d: 231 (properly s.),
    d: 233
Leton, br. Roger. canon of
    Haughmond d: 219, p: 224
letters dimissory, ordinations by virtue
    of 219–44, *passim*; for candidates
    from specified dioceses, see under the
    diocese
Levelerd (Leverlord), Isabella 204
    husband of *see* Langtre, Ralph de
Leykirke, Walter. r. Kedleston 73
Leylond, br. Ralph. monk of Croxden
    p: 243
Leyot, M. John. B.Dec. r. Bangor
    Iscoed 167
Leyot, M. Richard. v. St Michael,
    Coventry 62
    proctor for *see* Rodeley, Thomas
Leyot, Thomas 195
Lichefeld, br. Richard. canon of
    Repton p: 243
Lichefeld, br. William. canon of
    Wombridge s: 230, d: 231,
    p: 233
Lichfield [Lich'], Staffs, bp. of
    see Burghill, John; Catterick, John;
    Northburgh, Roger
    cathedral. archdeaconry in
        see Stafford
    canons of *see* Barton, M. Thomas;
        Bullok, M. Walter; Catterick,
        Robert; Crosseby, Nicholas; Forest,
        John; Goldeston, M. William;
        Holbache, M. Hugh; Neweport,
        M. William; Newhagh, M. William;
        Parys, M. Maior; Piers, Walter;
        Turvill, Philip
    chapel of St Mary 185
    chapter house, document dated at
        218
    dean of *see* Stretton, Thomas de
    dean and chapter of 37, 104, 110,
        121, 218
        act books of xi–xii
        pension payable to 32
    documents dated at 215, 217
    ordinations in 219, 221–2, 224,
        226–8, 230–44
prebends in *see* Bishops Itchington,
    Bobenhull, Eccleshall, Freeford,
    Longdon, Prees, Ryton, Ufton
    Cantoris
prebendaries of *see* Lichfield
    cathedral, canons of
precentor of *see* Wolden, Robert
treasurer of xii *see also* Barton,
    M. Thomas
chapel of St Mary in the Square 223
consistory court of 81
seal of Officiality of 4, 23, 81, 107, 169,
    186, 189, 194–6, 198–200, 204–9,
    211, 214–18
documents dated at 2–4, 7–21, 23,
    25–7, 31, 50, 55, 64, 66–8, 70–4,
    77–8, 81–2, 85–7, 89–91, 102–3,
    115, 120, 127, 130, 155, 163, 169,
    186, 188–90, 192–5, 198–201,
    203–8, 210–14, 216
Franciscans of *see* Bowell, William;
    Bradkirke, Edward; Brendurgas, Ed.;
    Bromwich, Thomas; Colonia,
    Antony de; Colonia, Henry de;
    Colonia, Sibertus de; Denton, Henry;
    Holt, John; Musche, John; Newton,
    Louis; Pole, Maurice; Trevers, John;
    Walsale, John; Wenlock, John
hospital of St John the Baptist,
    ordinands to title of *see* Farynton,
    Laurence; Harley, William; Mos,
    Richard; Shukbourgh, Thomas;
    Spicer, Richard
Lilbourne, Northants, vicarage of xii
Lilleshall [Lillushill, Lillushull, Lyllushill,
    Lyllushull], Salop, abbot and convent
    of 139
    canons of *see* Beston, William;
    Hagno, Thomas; Prync, Thomas
    ordinands to title of *see* Busch, John;
    Hadenall, Thomas; Ipstones,
    Nicholas; Jeykyn, Philip; Milner,
    Geoffrey; Offeley, John; Parker,
    William; Pyrton, John; Staunden,
    Thomas
Lillyng, Thomas. v. Ault Hucknall,
    v. Wysall 85–6
Lincoln, Lincs. bp. of *see* Repingdon,
    Philip
    cathedral. canon of *see* Forest, John
    chancellor of *see* Duffeld, M. Thomas
    dean of *see* Macworth, M. John

Lincoln, Lincs. – *contd.*
　　prebend in　*see* Sutton le Marsh
　　prebendary of　*see* Duffeld,
　　　M. Thomas
　diocese, ordinands from　*see* Barton,
　　Robert; Brabson, Richard; Brabson,
　　Thomas; Braybon, Richard; Childe,
　　Robert; Forst, Thomas; Hachet,
　　William; Hosier, Robert; Idell,
　　William; Kyng, John; Langford, Iblo;
　　Morgan, John; Piers, Thomas; Pole,
　　John; Porter, William; Rose, Robert;
　　Salman, Thomas; Spencer, Hugh;
　　Spicer, Richard; Tailour, John;
　　Wethenale, Thomas; Wynslowe,
　　Richard
　hospital of St Katherine, ordinand to
　　title of　*see* Grossefeld, William
Little Gidding　*see* Gidding, Little
Llanfachairn [Lanbechyn, Landbechyn,
　Llanvechyn], Montgom,
　rectory 145–7
　rectors of　*see* Bouch, M. John;
　　Wicherley, Thomas
Llandewi-Brefi [Llandewibredy,
　Llandewythbredy], Cardig, canon
　of　*see* Legburn, William
Lodlowe, br. Thomas. monk of
　Shrewsbury　p: 231
Loghtborowe (Loughteborowe,
　Loughtebourgh), br. John. monk of
　Charley 188
London, Midd. bp. of　*see* Clifford,
　Richard
　church of St Michael Cornhill. chantry
　　at altar of Blessed Virgin Mary for
　　Newcomen family 38–40
　priests of　*see* Bote, John;
　　Whiteacre, John
　documents dated at　xi, 38, 177
London, br. Thomas, monk of
　Coventry　s: 224, s: 225 (properly
　d.)　p: 236
London, William　d:219
Longdon, Staffs. prebend in Lichfield
　cathedral. prebendary of
　see Neweport, M. William
　prebendal vicarage　xii, 121
　vicar of　*see* Lyot, Thomas
Longdon, John　s: 242, d: 243, p: 244
Longford, Derb. rector of　*see* Radclif,
　Richard de

vicarage　67
vicar of　*see* Hayward, Roger
Longford　*see* Langford
Longlee, John. chantry chaplain at
　Bedworth　36
　proctor for　*see* Stonley, Thomas
Longley, Robert, esq.　159
Longley, Stephen de　a: 244
Longley, Thurstan de. r. Prestwich　159,
　a: 224, s: 225, d: 236, d: 237
　(properly p.)
Longnore (Langnore), Richard　d: 234,
　p: 236
Loppington [Lopyngton, Lopynton],
　Salop, vicarage　129
　vicars of　*see* Duffelt, John; Ellesmer,
　Roger
Loughteborowe, Loughtebourgh
　see Loghtborowe
Love, John　s: 239, d: 240, p: 242
Lovell, lady　*see* Lovell, Matilda
Lovell, Matilda, lady Lovell and
　Holand　154
Lowe, br. David. canon of Norton　d: 231
　(properly s.), d: 233, p: 238
Lowe, John (once Thomas)　s: 225,
　d: 226, p: 227
Lowe, Thomas　a: 240
Loweles, William　s: 242, d: 243, p: 244
Lowthe, John de. r. Blore, r. mediety of
　Treswell　115–16
Loxley, Thomas　a and s: 244
Ludlow [Ludlowe], Salop, hospital of St
　John, ordinand to title of
　see Temside, John
Lutley [Lutteley], Staffs, Isabella, lady
　of　123
Lye, br. John　a: 239
Lye, Philip. chantry pt. of St James in
　Hillmorton church　59
Lye, Roger　d: 228, p: 229 (?same as
　Robert Lelye)
Lymm [Lymne], Ches, rectory of mediety
　of　156
　rector of　*see* Dunvile, Roger
Lyne, Richard　a: 228, s: 229, d: 230, p: 2.
Lyne, Robert　s: 232, d: 233, p: 234
Lyot, Thomas. prebendal v.
　Longdon　121
Lytster, Robert. r. Wistaston, r.
　Ashton-on-Mersey　180–1
　proctor for　*see* Spiser, Richard

Macworth, M. John. dean of Lincoln   79,
   81
Madak, Richard   212
Malka (Malcane), Richard   a: 233,
   s: 234, d: 235, p: 237
Malpas, Hugh del, esq.   181
Mankok (Mankoc, Monkoc), Hugh
   a: 232, s: 239, d: 240, p: 242
Mantua, Italy, documents dated at   215,
   217
Marchall, Henry   a: 231
Mariot   see Maryot
Markby [Markeby], Lincs, ordinand to title
   of   see Wright, William
Markyate [Lesco iuxta Marke3ate], Beds,
   prioress and convent of   20
Marley, br. John   p: 221
Marny, Thomas, knt   177, 179
marriage   199, 202
   clandestine   see also dispensations
Maryot (Mariot), John. dean of Astley,
   v. Swalcliffe   55–7
Marys, br. John   a: 243
Mason, John. v. Newnham   31
Mason, Ranulf. v. in St John, Chester
   s: 237
Mason, William. v. Alstone   102
Massam, William   s: 239, d: 240, p: 241
Massy, Richard   s: 244
Massy, William le, son of Hamo
   le   186–7
   wife of   see Werburton, Petronilla de
Mathewe, William   200
Mautravers, lord   see Arundell, John
Maxstoke [Maxstok], Warw, canons
   of   see Grene, John; White, John
Maynwaryng, Ranulf   168
Mead, Kings, Derb, ordinands to title
   of   see Ronyngton, John; Tapley,
   William; Wyndyn, Christopher
Medburne, Thomas. incumbent of South
   Wingfield   72
Meghhen (Meghen), William   s: 239,
   d: 240, p: 242
Melbourne [Melburn], St Michael, Derb.
   chantry of St Katherine   88
   priest of   see Thurnaston, John
   vicarage   70
   vicar of   see Wylton, William de
Melbourne, br. Robert. canon of Church
   Gresley   s: 221, d: 222, p: 237
Merevale [Miravall, Miravalle], Warw.

monks of   see Atherston, John;
   Preston, Robert
ordinand to title of   see Newman, John
Merland, Henry   s: 227, d: 228
Merser, William   a: 232
Mesch, Cecilia de le   202
   kinswoman of   see Wynstanley,
   Emmote de
Milde, br. John, O.P., of
   Shrewsbury   d: 219
Milner, Geoffrey   s: 240, d: 242, p: 243
Milverton, Warw, prebend of, in Astley
   church   42
   prebendary of   see Cristenmasse,
   M. Thomas
Milward, Geoffrey   a: 232
Molyngton (Molynton), John   198
Molyngton, John   a: 227, s: 228, d: 229,
   p: 230
money, theft of   200
Monford, William. lord of Coleshill   13
Monk Bretton   see Bretton, Monk
Monkoc   see Mankoc
Montford [Monford], Salop,
   vicarage   140, 143
   vicars of   see Hamon, Richard;
   Pullurbage, Roger; Wri3t, Thomas
More, Henry   s: 244
More, br. John del. monk of Whalley
   p: 224
More, br. Thomas. monk of Burton
   s: 219, d: 220, p: 233
Moreton   see Morton
Morgan (Morgon), John   s: 225, d: 226,
   p: 227
Morgan, M. Philip. I.U.D. incumbent of
   Prescot   157
   proctor for   see Fulham, br. John
Morley, Ralph de   a: 227, s: 232, d: 233,
   p: 238
Morton, Derb, rectory   82–3
   rectors of   see Asshebery, William;
   Hynton, John de
Morton (Moreton), br. John. canon of
   Baswich   s: 220, d: 221, p: 232
Morton, Roger. incumbent of
   Clowne   95
Mos (Mosse), Richard   s: 231, d: 232,
   p: 233
Mos, Richard   s: 237, d: 238, p: 239
Mugginton [Mogynton], Derb, rectory of
   mediety of   107

Mugginton [Mogynton] – *contd.*
 rectors of   *see* Gybones, Roger;
  Reynald, John
Mulfield, Robert. bp. Killalo   226–44
Musche, br. John, O.F.M., of
  Lichfield   p: 243
Mustelwike (Mustulwike), br. William
  (once John), O.E.S.A., of
  Atherstone   s: 240, d: 241, p: 242

Nailstone [Naylstone], Leics, r. of
  see Langford, Iblo
Napton, br. Richard. canon of
  Kenilworth   p: 225
Nennewik   *see* Nonnewyk
Neston, br. Richard   s: 242
Neston, br. Thomas, O.F.M.   a: 226
Netham, John   s: 229
Neuport,   *see* Neweport
Neuton   *see* Newton
Newcastle under Lyme [Novum Castrum],
  Staffs, Dominican of   *see* Langford,
  William
Newcastle upon Tyne [Novum Castrum
  super Tynam], Northumb, St
  Nicholas. vicarage   50–2
 vicars of   *see* Glym, M. William;
  Thresk, Robert de
Newcomen, Robert, and Matilda and
  Petronilla, his wives, chantry for
  see London, St Michael Cornhill,
  chantry at altar of Blessed Virgin
  Mary for Newcomen family
Neweport (Neuport, Newport),
  M. Gregory. prebendal v. of
  Eccleshall, incumbent of Church
  Lawford   26, 120
Neweport, M. William. prebendary of
  Longdon, keeper of spiritualities *sede*
  vacante   x, 121
Neweson (Newesone), Thomas   115, 117
Newhagh, M. William. canon of
  Lichfield   185
Newman, John   a: 224, s: 225, d: 226,
  p: 227
Newnham [Newenham], Warw,
  vicarage   31
 vicars of   *see* Mason, John; Wright,
  Thomas
Newport   *see* Neweport
Newson (Nuson), br. John, O.Carm., of
  Coventry   d: 224, p: 225

Newstead in Sherwood, Notts, prior and
  convent of   86
Newton Purcell [Newenton Purcell],
  Oxon, rectory   27–9
 rectors of   *see* Flessher, Thomas; Islep,
  John
Newton (Neuton), br. John, canon of
  Repton   s: 232, d: 233
Newton, br. Louis, O.F.M., of
  Lichfield   d: 226, p: 227
Newton, Reginald   a: 238
Nonnewyk (Nennewik, Nonnwyk), br.
  Roger de. monk of Whalley   s: 224,
  d: 230, p: 231
Norbury, Staffs. lord of   *see* Boteler,
  Philip
 rectory   111
  rector of   *see* Russell, William
Normanton, John   s: 236, d: 237, p: 238
Normanton, Robert   s: 226, d: 227,
  p: 228
Northampton, Northants. Dominican
  of   *see* Herford, Geoffrey
 Franciscans of   *see* Langford, Richard;
  Rothewell, William; Suderman, John
 hospital of St John the Baptist,
  ordinands to title of   *see* Forst,
  Thomas; Idell, William
Northampton, br. John. monk of
  Coventry   s: 224, s: 225 (sic)
Northburgh, Roger. bp. of Lichfield,
  register of   x
Northenden [Northden, Northeden],
  Ches, church   174
 incumbent of   *see* Spark, Roger
Northmoor [More], Oxon, rector of
  see Clayton, Henry
North Wingfield   *see* Wingfield, North
Norton, Ches, canons of   *see* Coton,
  William; Coton, William; Lee,
  Henry de; Lowe, David; Torfote,
  Henry
Norton, John. v. Eccleshall   201
Norton, br. Thomas. monk of Burton
  s: 219, d: 220, p: 233
Norwich [Norwicum], Norf. bp. of
  see Wakeryng, John
 church of St Peter, Northgate.
  rectory   23
  rectors of   *see* Palmer, William;
  Tudde, John
 document dated at   23

notarial instruments 215, 217
notaries public *see* Barbour, M. John;
    Duffeld, M. Robert; Forbour,
    M. William
Nottingham [Notyngham], Notts,
    Franciscans of *see* John; Jacobi,
    Cornelius
Nowell, John a: 224, d: 227, p: 231
Nuneaton [Nunneton], Warw, ordinand
    to title of *see* Bosvyll, Richard
Nuson *see* Newson

obedience, oath of 185
Offchurch [Offechurch, Offechurche],
    Warw, vicarage 7–8, 25
    vicars of *see* Carix, Reginald; Ruhale,
    Hugh
Offeley, John a: 224, s: 226, d: 227,
    p: 228
Old Ford *see* Ford, Old
Onne (Orme), Thomas de a: 227, s: 229,
    d: 231, p: 232
Oreton, David de 196
Orme *see* Onne
Orsini, Jordan. bp. of Albano, papal
    penitentiary 186, 188–99, 202–6,
    210–17
    substitute for *see* Ponte, Anthony de
Osbarn (Osborn), John. v. Cound, r. or
    warden of Kingston Russell 130–1
    proctor for *see* Fairford, Henry
Oteley, John s: 238, d: 239, p: 241
Overton, David de s: 229, d: 230
Overton, William. r. Stirchley 133
Owston [Osolveston, Ossolveston,
    Osvoldeston, Osvolveston], Leics,
    ordinands to title of *see* Kyng, John;
    Tuy, Thomas
Oxford [Oxon'], Oxon. Franciscan of
    see Yonge, Matthew
    hospital of St John the Baptist outside
    the east gate 45
    St Frideswide, ordinand to title of
    see Clayton, William
    Winchester college 55, 57

Pach, John s: 221, d: 224, p: 225
Packington, Great [Magna Pakynton,
    Pakyngton, Pakynton], Warw,
    vicarage 4–6, 15–17
    vicars of *see* Hervy, William;
    Racheford, John; Shylton, John

Palmer, William. r. Elmdon, r. St Peter,
    Northgate, Norwich 23
Parker (Parke), Hugh s: 242, d: 243,
    p: 244
Parker, Richard a: 228, s: 230, d:231,
    p: 232
Parker, William a: 227, s: 230, d: 231,
    p: 232
Parys, M. Maior. prebendary of Bobenhull
    in Lichfield cathedral 218
Parys, br. Robert. monk of Whalley
    p: 224
Patching [Pacchyng], Sussex, rector
    of *see* Trewman, John
patrimony, ordinand to title of *see* Bolde,
    M. William
Payn, Thomas. chaplain of Sibthorpe
    college 82, 84
Pecche, John, esq. 38, 40
Peche, William a: 236
Peldon, Essex, rectory 177, 179
    rectors of *see* Saxy, John; Tebbot,
    Edmund
Pemburton, Thurstan de 202
    wife of *see* Wynstanley, Emmote de
Penbrugg, Isabella, widow of Fulk,
    knt. 138
penitentiary, papal *see* Orsini, Jordan;
    Ponte, Anthony de
    seal of 212–13, 215, 217
Penkridge [Pencrich, Pencrych], Staffs.
    document dated at 107
    royal free chapel. dean of *see* Cranley,
    Thomas; commissary or lieutenant
    of *see* Cranley, Thomas
    prebend in 107; prebendaries
    of *see* Gybones, Roger: Reynald,
    John
    seal of jurisdiction of 107
Pennesby, Richard a: 243
pension. from church, to dean and chapter
    of Lichfield 32
    ordination of 209
Pent, Robert. v. Clifton on
    Dunsmore 54
Penyale, Hugh. v. Crich 98
Penynton, Hugh 214
Pepepoynt, br. Ralph. monk of
    Upholland s: 238
Perepoynt, br. Laurence. monk of
    Upholland (same as above?) a: 236,
    d: 243

Person, William. v. Dilhorne, v.
    Caverswall   104, 126
Perton   *see* Pyrton
Pesale, Adam de, knt.   41
Peynter (Peyntour), br. John, O.E.S.A.,
    of Atherstone   s: 240, d: 242, p: 243
Philippi, John, of Egerton   199
    wife of   *see* Waryn, Margaret
Piers, Thomas   s: 240, d: 242, p: 243
Piers, Walter. canon of Lichfield   185
Pipewell [Pypewell], Northants. ordinands
    to title of   *see* Childe, Robert;
    Salman, Thomas
    rector of   *see* Curson, Thomas
Pirton   *see* Pyrton
Pitchford [Pycheford], Derb. church   127
    incumbent of   *see* Conede, Thomas
Pleasley [Pleseley], Derb. church   96
    incumbent of   *see* Takell, M. Roger
    lord of   *see* Haxey, Thomas
Plummer, M. John. incumbent of
    Tattenhall   162
Pole, John. r. mediety of Walton, v.
    Baschurch   151–3, a: 230, s: 231,
    d: 236, p: 237
Pole, M. John. incumbent of
    Brailsford   77
Pole, br. Maurice, O.F.M., of
    Lichfield   s: 221, d: 222
Polesworth [Pollesworth], Warw. abbess
    and convent of   60
    ordinands to title of   *see* Baker, Robert;
    Prest, John
    vicarage   60
    vicar of   *see* West, John
Pollesworth, br. Thomas. monk of
    Coventry   s: 224, s: 225 (sic)
Ponte, Anthony de. bp. of Concordia,
    acting papal penitentiary   205–8,
    212–15, 217
pope   *see* Clement VI, John XXIII
Pope, Thomas   s: 227, d: 231
Porter, Roger   200
Porter, William   s: 232, d: 233, p: 236
Potter (Pottere), Nicholas. r.
    Coddington   155
Potter, Roger   s: 225, d: 226, p: 227
Power, Roger. v. Heath   101
Prees [Prise], Salop, prebend in Lichfield
    cathedral   xi
    prebendary of   *see* Forest, John
    prebendal vicarage of   109–10

vicars of   *see* Admondeston, Thomas;
    Corley, William
Presbury   *see* Prestbury
Prescot [Prestecote], Lancs, church   157
    incumbent of   *see* Morgan, M. Philip
Prest, John   a: 234, s: 243, p: 244
Prestbury, Ches, vicarage   160
    vicars of   *see* Duncalf, John; Shagh,
    John del
Prestbury (Presbury), William de   s: 241,
    d: 242, p: 243
Preston, br. Robert. monk of
    Merevale   p: 219
Preston, William   a: 240
Prestwich, Lancs, rectory   159
    rector of   *see* Longley, Thurstan de
Prestwode, William. master of St
    Thomas's hospital, Birmingham   30
Pris   *see* Prys
Prise, Richard   s: 243
prison, bishop's   200–1
Prossell, Thomas   a: 239
Prymmerose (Prymrose), Richard   a: 237,
    s: 238, d: 239, p: 242
Prync, br. Thomas. canon of Lilleshall
    s: 242
Prys (Pris), John   s: 229, d: 230, p: 231
Pullurbage, Roger. v. Montford   143
Pyrton (Perton, Pirton), John   s: 227,
    d: 228, p: 230

Racheford, John. v. Leek Wootton   46
Racheford, John. v. Great Packington,
    master of Wyham college and Cadeby
    chapel   4–6
Radbourn [Rodbourne], Warw,
    church   44
    incumbent of   *see* Steward, John
Radclif (Radclyf, Raddecliff, Radeclif,
    Radeclyf), Alice de   217
    husband of   *see* Chernok, Ranulf alias
    Houkyn de
Radclif, George de. r. Wilmslow   166,
    182
Radclif, John de   s: 236, d: 237, p: 238
Radclif, Ralph son of Ralph de, knt.   192
    wife of   *see* Graven, Cecilia
Radclif, Richard de. r. Longford   67
Radclif, Robert de   166
    Joan, wife of   166
Radway [Radeway, Radeweye], Warw,
    vicarage   33, 48

vicars of *see* Reynald, William;
   Watton, Richard
Ranton [Ronton], Staffs, prior and
   convent of 34
   ordinands to title of *see* Adyns, John;
   Cowley, Thomas; Cronage, Thomas;
   Goodman, Roger; Heyr, John;
   Kemsay, William; Onne, Thomas de;
   Siryth, Thomas; Stevenson, Thomas,
   Wolaston, John
Rasyn, br. John, O.S.A./O.P., of
   Stafford s: 234, d: 238, p: 239
Raynforth (Raynford), Thomas s: 237,
   d: 238, p: 239
Rede, Edward s: 221, d: 222, p: 224
Rede, Edward. r. Yoxall d: 229, p: 230
regular orders (no house or order given),
   ordinands from *see* Arnall, John;
   Barnvil, Richard; Chatburn,
   Nicholas; Cleydon, John; Clifton,
   Thomas; Deyne, John; Fulham,
   Denis; Flynt, Denis; Hawes, William;
   Holkote, Bartholomew; Hunt,
   Walter; Kirkham, John; London,
   Thomas: Lye, John; Marley, John;
   Marys, John; Neston, Richard
religious, as incumbents 97, 99
Rendant, Robert s: 236
Repingdon (Repyndon, Repdon), br.
   John. canon of Repton s: 232, d:
   233
Repingdon, Philip. bp. of Lincoln xii,
   4–5, 12–13, 15–16, 18–19, 27,
   55–6, 74, 78, 91, 151–3
Repton [Repyndon], Derb. canons of
   see Harley, John; Lichefeld, Richard;
   Newton, John; Repyndon, John
   ordinands to title of *see* Boseworth,
   William; Elyot, John; Fissher,
   William; Love, John; Morley, Ralph
   de; Parker, Richard; Roges, John;
   Spencer, John; Whitesith, Henry
Repyndon *see* Repingdon
Reresby, Thomas, knt. 65
Reresby, William. incumbent of
   Ashover 65
Rewley [Regali loco], Oxon, ordinand to
   title of *see* Netham, John
Reynald, John. r. mediety of Mugginton,
   prebendary in Penkridge royal free
   chapel 107
Reynald, William. v. Radway 48

Ricard, Richard a: 220
Richard, monk of Burton p: 228
Rideley, br. Louis, O.P., of
   Shrewsbury p: 219
Rider, Alan 200
Ridware, Staffs, John Coton of, q.v.
Rissheton, br. William. canon of
   Haughmond s: 225, p: 238
Robert (witness) 217
Roby, John s: 236, d: 237, p: 238
Robyns, John a: 226, s: 231, d: 232,
   p: 233
Robyns, John a: 232, s: 238, d: 239,
   p: 240
Robyns, Thomas s: 244
Robynton, John a: 227
Rocester [Roucester, Roucestre], Staffs.
   canons of *see* Bromeley, John;
   Brompton, Robert; Hanbury, John;
   Smyth, William
   ordinands to title of *see* Broun, John;
   Twenbrokus, Richard; Verney,
   Philip; Waterfall, John;
   Wyndesovere, John
Rodeley, Thomas. proctor for M. Richard
   Leyot 62
Rodington [Rodyngton], Salop, free
   chapel 137
   chaplain of *see* Chirbury, William
Roges, John s: 225
Rolf, John. r. Wishaw, v. Hathersage
   21
Rolleston, William de, esq. 107
Rolleston, William. lord of
   Swarkeston 89
Ronton *see* Ranton
Ronyngton, John s: 239, d: 241, p: 242
Rose, Robert s: 226, d: 227, p: 228
Ross Hall [Rossale], Salop. chapel.
   rectory 141
   rectors of *see* Felton, William;
   Walleford, William
   lord of *see* Yngelfeld, Philip
Rothewell, br. William, O.F.M., of
   Northampton p: 239
Rothley, Richard. abbot of St Mary,
   Leicester 169
Rotteley, br. Thomas. monk of
   Stoneleigh s: 231
Rugby [Rokeby], Warw, rectory 10
   rectors of *see* Hosell, Richard;
   Thurston, Thomas

Rugeley, br. Thomas. canon of Arbury
s: 219, d: 225, p: 238
Ruhale, Hugh. v. Offchurch, v.
Wolfhamcote 7–8, 25
Russell, William. r. Norbury 111
Russheton, Richard p: 219
Ruthin, lord of see Grey, Reginald de
Ruyton, William a: 236
Ryton, prebend in Lichfield cathedral xi

St Asaph, Wales, bp. of see Lancaster,
Robert
St Davids diocese, Wales, ordinand
from see Temside, John
Salbourne, dioc. London, chapel, warden
of see Bele, Richard
Salisbury [Sarum], Wilts. bp. of
see Hallum, Robert
cathedral, canon of see Crukadam,
M. Geoffrey
document dated at 130
seal of Officiality of 130
Salman, Thomas s: 225, d: 226, p: 227
Sandbach [Sandebache], Ches,
vicarage 172
vicar of see Hassale, Thomas
Sandiaker, William s: 225, d: 226,
p: 228
Sankey [Sonky], Lancs, Margaret daughter
of John Hycheson of, q.v.
Savage, John, clk. 210
Savage, John, knt. 119
Savage, John a: 233, s: 238, d: 244
Savage, Thomas. r. Checkley 119,
a: 233, s: 237, d: 244
Sawley [Sallay], Yorks, ordinand to title
of see Dugdale, Richard
Saxby, Leics, rectory 18, 20
rectors of see Bikenhill, William;
Croxale, Nicholas de
Saxby, William a: 236
Saxy, John. r. mediety of Wallasey,
r. Peldon 177–9
Scarcliffe [Scardeclyf], Derb, vicarage 64
vicar of see Elys, Gerard
Scaumsby (Scaunsby), Thomas s: 221,
d: 222, p: 224
Scawndon see Stavndon
Schagh, Ralph s: 242, d: 243
Scharyngton (Schiryngton), M. Henry.
r. Wappenbury 49, 63
Scheryngton, John 63

Schiryngton see Scharyngton
Schyngler see Shyngler
Scolys, Hugh s: 225, d: 226, p: 227
Scrayingham, Yorks, church xii
Screyfeld, William. v. Grandborough 34
seals see Barrow, William; Lichfield,
consistory; penitentiary, papal;
Penkridge, royal free chapel;
Salisbury, Officiality of
Selby [Silby, Silleby], Yorks, ordinand to
title of see Bolton, Thomas
Selby, br. John. canon of Beauchief
d: 237
Shagh, John del. v. Prestbury 160
Shardelowe, Geoffrey. second chantry
chaplain in Chaddesden chapel 100
Sharp, br. Stephen. monk of Combe
s: 239
Sheen [Shene], Surrey, Carthusians
of 12, 14, 113, 128, 134, 163, 165
Shelford, Notts, prior and convent of 69
ordinands to title of see Harden,
Robert; Stanley, William
Sheriff Hales [Shirifhales], Salop,
vicarage 113
vicar of see Lachefer, William
Sherman, Alexander. v. Clifton on
Dunsmore 9
Sherwood [Shirwode], Notts
see Newstead
Shipbrook [Shibbrok], Ches, Elizabeth
widow of Richard Vernon of, q.v.
Shiplond (Shiplode), br. Richard. canon
of Arbury s: 219, d: 237
Shirley, Thomas. v. Ilam 106
Shirwalacres, Henry s: 236, d: 237,
p: 238
Shiryngton, Robert. prebendary of
Wigginton in Tamworth
church 124
proctor for see Boton, John
Shrewsbury [Salop'], Salop. archdeaconry
of, institutions in 127–53
Dominicans of see Forest, Howell;
Milde, John; Rideley, Louis
St Chad. dean of collegiate church
of see Catterick, Robert
St Giles. hospital, ordinands to title
of see Bertton, William; Cay,
Thomas; Dawes, William; Lye,
Roger; Longdon, John; Longnore,
Richard; Lowe, John; Meghhen,

William; Pottere, Roger; Prise,
Richard; Prys, John; Rede, Edward;
Walker, John
St Peter. abbot and convent of   136–7,
146, 148, 150, 152, 209
monks of   see Aston, John;
Ideshale, Roger; Lodlowe, Thomas;
Wode, John
Shukbourgh, Thomas   s: 226
Shylton, John. v. Great Packington, v. St
Nicholas, Leicester   15–17
Shyngler (Schyngler), Thomas   s: 219,
d: 220, p: 224
Sibthorpe [Sibthorp], Notts, college or
chantry of St Mary. chaplain of
see Payn, Thomas
mastership of   82–4
masters of   see Asshebery,
William; Hynton, John de
Siryth, Thomas   d: 219
Sleaford [Sleford], Lincs, castle,
documents dated at   4, 12, 15, 18,
27, 55, 74, 78, 151
Smethurst (Smethyrst), John   s: 224,
d: 225, p: 226
Smyth, Adam   a: 232, s: 244
Smyth, John   a: 238
Smyth, Richard   s: 244
Smyth, Thomas   s: 230, d: 231, p: 232
Smyth, William. incumbent of
Harborough Magna   41
Smyth, William   191
Smyth, William. v. Clifton on
Dunsmore   54
Smyth, William   s: 225, d: 226, p: 227
Smyth, William. canon of Rocester
s: 232, d: 233
Snell, John   a: 239, s: 241, d: 242, p: 243
Snowe, John   a: 242
Sondon, Nicholas. r. Kingsley   118
Sonky (Sonke), Gilbert   d: 219, p: 220
Sonky, Robert   190
Sonky, Robert   a: 231, s: 232, p: 234
Sotheworth, John   a: 239, s: 240, d: 241,
p: 242
Southam, Warw, rectory   32
pension from to dean and chapter of
Lichfield   32
rectors of   see Besevill, M. John;
Sturdy, Robert
Southam, br. John. canon of
Kenilworth   d: 225

Southam, br. John. canon of
Kenilworth   d: 236, p: 242
Southwell [Southewell], Notts, St Mary,
ordinands to title of   see Bewford,
John; Pope, Thomas
South Wingfield   see Wingfield, South
Sparham [Sperham], Norf, rector of
see Inse, William
Spark, Roger. incumbent of
Northenden   174
Spencer, Hugh   a: 232, s: 233, d: 234, p: 236
Spencer, John   a: 233, s: 236, d: 237, p: 238
Spicer (Spycer), Richard, of Foxton,
Leics   p: 219
Spicer, Richard   a: 231, s: 232, d: 233,
p: 234
Spiser, Richard   181
Spycer   see Spicer
Spyne (Spyney), br. Robert, O.Carm., of
Coventry   s: 226, d: 230
Spynk (Spynke), John. r. Aughton,
r. Freshwater   163–4
Stacy, Thomas. v. Horsley   90
Stafford, Staffs. archdeaconry of   122
archdeacon of   see Fytton, M. John
institutions to benefices in   102–26
Augustinians of   see Dalton, Richard;
Desford, John; Forbrig, Laurence;
Rasyn, John
Dominicans of   see Forbrig, Laurence;
Rasyn, John
justices at   200
St John, hopital of near, ordinand to title
of   see Travell, James
St Thomas, monastery of near
see Baswich
Stafford, Edmund. bp. of Exeter, lord of
Clifton Campville   103, 125
Stafford, M. John, professor of civil law.
r. Clifton Campville   103
Stafford, br. Philip. canon of Stone
a: 239, s: 240, d: 242, p: 243
Stafford, Richard, knt., son and heir
of   see Stafford, Edmund
Standon [Staundon], Staffs, church   200
rector of   see Boydell, Henry
Stanley, Ralph/Ranulf   a: 221, s: 222,
d: 224, p: 225
Stanley, M. Richard. incumbent of
Alderley, r. Walton on the
Hill   158, 173
proctor for   see Iremonger, John

Stanley, William   s: 220, d: 221, p: 222
Stanton upon Hine Heath [Stanton,
    Staunton], Salop, vicarage   144
  vicars of   *see* Don, John: Falk, Henry
Stanton, br. Robert, O.Carm. of
    Coventry   d: 225
Stanyhirst   *see* Stanyhurst
Stanyhurst (Stanyhirst), Thomas   s: 242,
    d: 243, p: 244
Stapulforth, John. v. Ault Hucknall,
    v. Wysall   85–7
Staresmore, Robert   s: 244
Stavndon (Scawndon, Staundon),
    Thomas   s: 225, s: 226 (properly d.),
    p: 227
Stavnford, br. John, O.Carm., of
    Coventry   a: 225
Stedman, Roger. incumbent of Eyam   68
  proctor for   *see* Haston, John
Stephene, John   a: 219
Stevenson (Stevynson), John   s: 225,
    d: 226, p: 228
Stevenson, Thomas   a: 231, s: 232,
    d: 233, p: 234
Steward, John. incumbent of
    Radbourn   44
Steyn, Thomas   a: 227, s: 228, d: 229,
    p: 230
Stirchley [Stirchesley], Salop,
    rectory   133
  rectors of   *see* Overton, William;
    Wyeghus, Richard
Stockes, John, bp. of Kilmore   219
Stockton [Stokton], Warw,
    rectory   38–40
  rectors of   *see* Bote, John: Whiteacre,
    John
Stoke, Thomas   a: 243
Stokton, Ralph   a: 229
Stone, Staffs. canon of   *see* Stafford,
    Philip
  ordinand to title of   *see* Claybrok,
    Richard
Stoneleigh [Stonley, Stonleya], Warw.
    abbot and convent of   33, 48
  monks of   *see* Caudray, William;
    Coudray, William; Rotteley,
    Thomas; Stonley, Thomas; White,
    John; Worsop, William
  ordinands to title of   *see* Clyfton,
    William; Gerard, William; Heyne,
    William; Smyth, Richard

vicarage   35
  vicar of   *see* Clyfton, William
Stonley, br. John, canon. v. Kirk
    Hallum   99
Stonley, br. Thomas. monk of
    Stoneleigh   d: 237
Stonley, Thomas. proctor for John
    Longlee   36
Straunge, John. r. Bangor Iscoed   167
Stretton, John   a: 227
Stretton, Thomas de. dean of
    Lichfield   218
Strickland, William. bp. of Carlisle   50,
    52, 70
Stronge, Robert   217
Sturdy, Robert. r. Southam   32, a: 225,
    s: 231, d: 235, p: 236
Suderman, br. John, O.F.M., of
    Northampton   d: 239
Sulby [Selby, Silbi, Silby], Northants, St
    Mary, ordinands to title of
    see Brabson, Richard: Brabson,
    Thomas; Braybon, Richard;
    Swynburn, Thomas; Wethenale,
    Thomas
Sumter, John   177, 179
Surrey, archdeacon of   *see* Forest, John
suspension of priest   199
Sutte, Richard   a: 231
Sutton le Marsh [Sutton in le Merssh],
    Lincs, prebend in Lincoln cathedral.
    prebendary of   *see* Duffeld, M.
    Thomas
  prebendal vicarage   78–80
    vicars of   *see* Fouler, John;
    Fridaythorp alias Clerk, John
Sutton Scarsdale [Sutton in le Dale], Derb,
    church   94
  incumbent of   *see* Kyrke, John by the
Sutton, Henry   s: 224
Sutton, br. Henry. canon of Dale   s: 226,
    d: 227
Sutton, br. Thomas, O.P., of Warwick
    s: 225
Swalcliffe [Sualcliff, Sualclyf, Swalclyf,
    Swalclyff], Oxon, vicarage   55, 57
  vicars of   *see* Maryot, John; Wildebore,
    Nicholas
Swarkeston [Swerkeston], Derb.
    church   89
  incumbent of   *see* Dauntre, Thomas
  lord of   *see* Rolleston, William

Swepston, br. Richard, O.P., of
    Leicester p: 219
Swynburn, Thomas   d: 222
Swynley, Robert   a: 227, s: 231, d: 232,
    p: 233

Tailour, John   d: 233, p: 234
Tailour, John   a: 233, s: 234, d: 236,
    p: 237
Tailour, Juliane   200
Tailour, Richard   s: 239, d: 240, p: 242
Takell, M. Roger, LL.B. incumbent of
    Pleasley   96
Talbot, John, knt. lord Furnival   68
Tailboys, Walter   4, 6
Tamworth, Staffs, collegiate church,
    prebend in   see Wigginton
Tamworth, Richard   169
Tapley, William   s: 244
Tarlton, Reginald de   a: 222, s: 224,
    d: 225, p: 226
Tattenhall [Tatenhale], Ches,
    church   162
  incumbent of   see Bul, Richard;
    Plummer, M. John
Tebbot, Edmund. r. Peldon, r. mediety of
    Wallasey   177–8
Temside (Temsede, Temsete), John
    a: 232, s: 233, d: 234, p: 235
Tendryng, William, esq.   177, 179
Teye, Robert, esq.   177, 179
Thakar, Thomas   s: 228, d: 230, p: 231
Thake, Thomas   a: 220
theft   200–1
Thelsford [Telesford, Telisford], Warw, St
    Radegunde, ordinand to title of
    see Hill, Robert
Thorpe Constantine [Thorp Constantyn],
    Staffs, rectory   105
  rectors of   see Witherley, Richard;
    Witherley, William
Thresk, Robert de. v. St Nicholas,
    Newcastle-upon-Tyne; v. St Michael,
    Coventry   50–2
  proctor for   see Burton, John
Thurnaston, John. chantry pt. of St
    Katherine in St Michael,
    Melbourne   88
Thurston, Thomas. r. Rugby   10
Tildesley, Ranulf de   s: 244
Tolle, Richard   a: 238
Tolle, Robert   s: 242, d: 243, p: 244

Toneworth, William. r. Dalbury, r. Little
    Gidding   74–6
Tong [Tonge], Salop, college of St
    Bartholomew, wardenship of   138
  warden of   see Admondeston, M.
    William
Toppyng, Henry   s: 237, d: 238, p: 239
Torefote (Torfote), br. Henry, canon of
    Norton   d: 231 (properly s.)
    d: 233, p: 238
Travell, James   a: 220, s: 222, d: 223,
    p: 224
Trentham, Staffs. canon of   see Aldelem,
    Alexander
  ordinands to title of   see Kefex,
    Richard; Mankok, Hugh
Treswell [Tireswell, Tyreswell], Notts,
    rectory of mediety of   115–17
  rectors of   see Halom, Robert; Lowthe,
    John de
Trevers, br. John, O.F.M., of Lichfield
    s: 237
Trewman, John. r. Patching   s: 237
Tripolitanensis, bp.   see Brampton, Simon
Trusbut, Peter. v. Crich   98
Tudde, John. r. Elmdon; r. St Peter,
    Northgate, Norwich   23
Turvill, Philip, chantry founded by
    see Bedworth
Tutbury [Tuttebury], Staffs, ordinands to
    title of   see Braybon, Laurence;
    Gibbons, John
Tuxford, Notts, church   xii
Tuy, Thomas   s: 243, d: 244
Twenbrokus, Richard (once Robert)
    s: 220, d: 221, p: 224
Tyler, William. chantry pt. in Hillmorton
    church   58

Ufton [Ulfton] Cantoris, Warw, prebend
    in Lichfield cathedral   37
  prebendaries of   see Crosseby,
    Nicholas; Holbache, M. Hugh
Upholland [Holand], Lancs. monks of
    see Burscogh, Nicholas; Pepepoynt,
    Ralph; Perepoynt, Laurence
  ordinands to title of   see Bowland,
    Robert; Coke, Henry; Dichefeld,
    Thomas; Fissher, James; Fissher,
    Robert; Hesketh, Gilbert de;
    Raynforth, Thomas
Ustanes (Evston), William   a: 243, s: 244

Vale Royal [Vale Regale, Valle Regali],
Ches. monk of *see* Lawe, Hugh
ordinands to title of *see* Belamy, John;
Beuglegh, Richard; Bone, John;
Broun, John; Hervy, Richard;
Prymmerose, Richard; Savage, John;
Sonky, Gilbert
Valle Crucis abbey, Denbighs. document
dated at 145
ordinand to title of *see* Wordulworth,
Roger
Vaudey [Valle Dei], Lincs, ordinand to
title of *see* Massy, Richard
Velleworth, Richard a: 239
Venables, Hugh de 192
wife of *see* Graven, Cecilia
Venables, John 208
Venables, Peter de 207
Venables, Richard 205
Venables, William 206
Verney, John. r. free chapels of Cuckow
Church and Wadborough a: 221,
s: 222, d: 223, p: 224
Verney, John a: 236
Verney, Philip (same as above?) s: 237,
d: 239, p: 240
Verney, William a: 234
Vernon, Elizabeth, widow of Richard of
Shipbrook, knt. 176
Vernon, br. Henry, O.S.A., of
Atherstone s: 231, d: 233, p: 240

Wadborough [Wardbarowe, Wardebargh,
Wardebarwe], Worcs, rector of *see*
Verney, John
Wade, Thomas a: 227, s: 230, d: 231,
p: 232
Wade *see also* Warde
Wakeryng, John. bp. of Norwich 23
vicar general for *see* Walsyngham,
James
Walbron, John. v. Market Drayton 128
Waldyns, Joanna. lady of Elmdon 23
Walkeden, John a: 236
Walker, John (once Thomas) a: 225,
s: 226, d: 232, p: 233
Walker, John a: 231, s: 233, d: 234,
p: 235
Walker, Thomas a: 240
Wall, Nicholas s: 238, d: 239, p: 242
Wallasey [Kirkebywaley in Walesey,
Kirkewaley, Kyrkebywaley], Ches,

rectory of mediety of 177–8
rectors of *see* Saxy, John; Tebbot,
Edmund
Walleford, William. r. Ross Hall 141
Walsale, br. John, O.F.M., of
Lichfield p: 230
Walsyngham, James 23
Walton, Bucks, rectory of mediety
of 151–3
rectors of *see* Bouch, M. John; Pole,
John
Walton on the Hill [Walton], Ches. rector
of *see* Stanley, M. Richard
vicarage 173
vicar of *see* Iremonger, John
Walton, Richard d: 219, p: 220
Walton, M. Thomas. prebendary in St
John, Chester; prebendary in St Mary
by the Castle, Leicester 169
Wappenbury [Wappynbury,
Wappyngbury], Warw, rectory 49,
63
rectors of *see* Bernard, John;
Scharyngton, M. Henry; Wroo,
William
Warde (Wade), Ed. s: 232, d: 236,
p: 237
Warde, Edward d: 219, p: 220
Warde, br. Nicholas. monk of Burton
s: 219, d: 220, p: 233
Warde, Richard p: 219
Waren *see* Waryn
Warmynton, Richard a: 244
Warrington [Weryngton], Lancs.
Augustinian of *see* Cressewell,
John; Dalton, Richard
Warwick (Warr'], Warw. Dominicans
of *see* Burton, Robert; Grant,
William; Huntar, Thomas; Sutton,
Thomas
St John the Baptist, hospital of,
ordinand to title of
see Lancastreshire, Thomas
St Mary, dean and chapter of 2, 8, 25
Waryn (Waren), Margaret Johannis 199
husband of *see* Philippi, John
Waryn, Richard a: 225, s: 226, d: 227,
p: 231
Waterfall (Waturhull), John s: 229,
d: 230, p: 231
Watton, Richard. v. Radway 33, 48
Waturhull *see* Waterfall

Wecherley see Wicherley
Welinton, John s: 237 (?same as John
  Belington)
Wellington [Welyngton], Salop,
  vicarage 150
house 209
  ordination of pension from 209
  vicars of see Grillushull, Thomas;
    Grillushull, William
Wells, Som, cathedral, chancellor of
  see Bruton, M. Richard
Wenlock [Wenlok], Salop. prior and
  convent of 133
  ordinand to title of see Walker, John
Wenlock (Wenlok), br. John, O.F.M., of
  Lichfield s: 232, d: 244
Weoley, Worcs, lord of see Burnell,
  Hugh
Wer (Were), Thomas atte s: 220, d: 221,
  p: 222
Werburton, Petronilla daughter of Richard
  de 186–7
  husband of see Massy, William le
Were see Wer
West, John. prebendal pt. of Wolvey
  Astley in Astley church 43
West, John. incumbent of Baddesley
  Clinton 47
West, John. v. Polesworth 60
West, John. r. Biscathorpe 4, 6
Westley, John a: 220, s: 222, d: 224,
  p: 225
Weston, Richard. v. Attingham 139
Wethenale (Widenale), Thomas a: 220,
  s: 224, d: 225, p: 226
Wetrev (Wetreve), Hugh a: 230, s: 231,
  d: 232, p: 233
Wexford, Ireland, lord of see Grey,
  Reginald de
Whalley [Whallay], Lancs. monks of
  see Bourgh, Richard; Clyderowe,
  Ralph; Dobnam, John de; Harden,
  Thomas de; More, John del;
  Nonnewyk, Roger de; Parys, Robert
  ordinands to title of see Belington,
  John; Blakelowe, Robert; Bolton,
  Henry de; Brid, John; Chedwike,
  John; Coventre, John de;
  Crossepeny, John; Fere, Adam de;
  Fleccher, John; Hatton, Laurence,
  de; Heton, John de; Hule, Thomas;
  Merland, Henry; Parker, Hugh;
  Radeclif, John de; Scolys, Hugh;
  Smethurst, John; Snell, John;
  Tailour, Richard; Welinton, John
Whatton, John. v. Clifton on Dunsmore 9
White, br. John. monk of Stoneleigh
  d: 225; d: 231 (properly p.)
White, br. John. canon of Maxstoke
  a: 236, s: 237, d: 239
Whiteacre, John. r. Stockton, chantry pt.
  in St Michael Cornhill, London 38–40
Whitesith, Henry s: 219, d: 220, p: 221
Whitlombe, Richard. r. Kedleston 73
Whitstone, Adam a: 244
Wicherley (Wecherley), Thomas. v.
  Baschurch, r. Llanfachairn 145–7
Widenale see Wethenale
Wigginton [Wiginton, Wigynton], Staffs,
  prebend in Tamworth church 124
  prebendary of see Shiryngton, Robert
Wildebore, Nicholas. dean of Astley, v.
  Swalcliffe 55–7
Willoughby [Welugby, Wylugby], Warw,
  vicarage 45
  vicars of see Bartlot, William;
    Garsyngton, John
Wilmslow [Wilmeslowe], Ches,
  rectory 166
  claimant of see Boseley, Geoffrey de
  disputed presentation to 182–4
  rectors of see Bothe, William de;
    Radclif, George de
Winchester [Wynton'], Hants. bp. of
  see Beaufort, Henry
  vicar general of see Forest, John
  cathedral, archdeacon of Surrey in
  see Forest, John
  document dated at 1
  St Cross near, document dated at 163
Wingfield, North [Northwynfeld], Derb,
  church 71
  incumbent of see Kyrkeman, Robert
Wingfield, South [Wynfeld], Derb,
  church 72
  incumbent of see Medburne, Thomas
Wishaw [Wysshawe], Warw, rectory 21
  rectors of see Clerc, William; Rolf, John
Wistaston [Wystaston], Ches,
  rectory 180–1
  rectors of see Bagelegh, William;
    Lytster, Robert
Witherley, Richard. r. Thorpe
  Constantine 105

Witherley, William. r. Thorpe
   Constantine   105, d: 233, p: 234
Wode, br. John. monk of Shrewsbury
   s: 236, d: 237, p: 242
Wode, Roger   a: 239
Wodehouse (Wodehous), John   a: 221,
   s: 229, d: 230, p: 231
Wodehouse, Richard. v. Albrighton   149
Wodelok (Wodeloke), John   a: 228,
   s: 229, d: 230, p: 231
Wodenassh, ordinand to title of
   see Rendant, Robert
Wolaston, John   p: 219
Wolaston, Richard   a: 233, s: 234,
   d: 235, p: 236
Wolden, Robert. precentor of Lichfield
   cathedral, prebendary of Bishops
   Itchington   28
Wolfall (Wollefall), Nicholas   s: 226,
   d: 227, p: 236
Wolfhamcote, Warw, vicarage   2, 7–8, 25
   vicars of   *see* Carix, Reginald;
   Hayward, Richard; Ruhale, Hugh
Wollefall   *see* Wolfall
Wolvey Astley   *see* Astley, Wolvey
Wombridge [Wombrug, Wombruge,
   Wombrugg, Wombrugge], Salop.
   canon of   *see* Lichefeld, William
   ordinands to title of   *see* Ade, John;
   Drayton, Thomas; Falke, Richard;
   Fraunces, Thomas; Hatton, John;
   London, William; Stevenson, John
   prior and convent of   129
Woodchurch [Wodechurch], Ches,
   rectory   175
   rectors of   *see* Coppenall, Thomas;
   Fouleshurst, Richard
wool, theft of   200
Worcester diocese, ordinand from
   see Hill, Robert
Wordulworth, Roger   s: 243
Wordworth, William   p: 219
Worksop [Wirkesope, Worsop], Notts,
   prior and convent of   85, 87, 95
   ordinand to title of   *see* Malcane,
   Richard
Worsop, br. William, monk of
   Stoneleigh   p: 222
Wotley, John   a: 237
Wouburn, John. r. Hanbury   114
Wright (Wryght), Thomas. v.
   Newnham   31

Wright, William   a: 220, s: 221, d: 222,
   p: 224
Wright, William   s: 229, d: 230, p: 231
writs, royal   183–4
Wriʒt, Thomas. v. Montford   140, 143
Wroo, William. r. Wappenbury   63
   proctor for   *see* Scheryngton, John
Wryght   *see* Wright
Wych, Richard   a: 231
Wyeghus, Richard. r. Stirchley   133
Wyham [Wyhom], Lincs, college,
   mastership of   4, 6
   masters of   *see* Hervy, William;
   Racheford, John
Wylton, William de. v. Melbourne   70
Wymark, John   a: 220, s: 221, d: 222,
   p: 224
Wyndehill   *see* Wyndhill
Wyndesovere, John   a: 231, d: 234,
   p: 236
Wyndhill (Wyndehill), John. r. Cound,
   r. or warden of Kingston
   Russell   130–2, 135
Wyndyn, Christopher   s: 244
Wynslowe, Richard   a: 232, s: 233,
   d: 236, p: 237
Wynstanley, Emmote de   202
   husband of   *see* Pemburton, Thurstan de
   kinswoman of   *see* Mesch, Cecilia de le
Wynwyk, Richard de. incumbent of
   Handley   171
Wysall [Wyshawe], Notts, vicarage   85–7
   vicars of   *see* Lillyng, Thomas;
   Stapulforth, John

Yngelfeld, Philip. lord of Ross Hall   141
Yonge, br. Matthew, O.F.M., of
   Oxford   p: 242
York, Yorks. abp. of   *see* Bowet, Henry
   diocese, ordinands from   *see* Bolton,
   Thomas; Coton, M. John; Fissher,
   John; Massam, William; Stanley,
   William; Wright, William
   document dated at   82
   Minster, dean and chapter of   81
   St Clement, ordinand to title of
   see Wright, William
Yoxall [Yoxale], Staffs, rector of
   see Rede, Edward

ʒerdley (ʒerdeley), br. Thomas. abbot of
   St Werburga, Chester   185